ST RY

Trading in Religion for Discipleship

by F. Barton Davis

WWW.JESUSLOVESTORY.COM

F. Barton Davis

Love Story

Trading in Religion for

Discipleship

www.jesuslovestory.com

Love Story

Published by Magi Media Publications

1675 Southpointe Dr.

Hoover Al 35244

Printed in the United States

Cover design: Brian Moore, Bmoe LLC

Interior design: Magi Media Publications

ISBN 978-0-9819502-5-9

To my lovely wife Michelle, my best friend and personal hero. You make me better and call me higher, through good times and bad. I thank God for blessing me with you and our special love and for our two amazing daughters, Jacquelyn and Kenya, who make our Love Story complete.

WWW.JESUSLOVESTORY.COM

Contents

Foreward   1

Chapter 1 **The End of Religion**   3

Chapter 2 **Formal Introductions**   9

Chapter 3 **The Love Letter**   25

Chapter 4 **Crazy In Love**   39

Chapter 5 **Being Exclusive**   53

Chapter 6 **The Engagement**   65

Chapter 7 **The Wedding**   85

Chapter 8 **Meet the Family**   98

Chapter 9 **Next Steps**   104

Bibliography   108

WWW.JESUSLOVESTORY.COM

Foreward

In his latest book, *Love Story*: Trading in Religion for Discipleship, Frank Davis utilizes the practical and powerful analogy of the "stages of a romantic relationship" to illustrate sound Biblical principles for becoming a true disciple of Jesus Christ. He states that *Spiritual Maturity* (learning to become disciples who make disciples) is the overall goal of the book. Personal illustrations from his own courtship with and marriage to Michelle help us understand and relate to ways in which intimacy and growth take place in our relationship with Christ.

Frank emphasizes the fact that being a true disciple is first and foremost (like in marriage) a personal relationship built on love for and commitment to Jesus Christ. His beautiful description in Chapter Three (Love Letter) of Christ's love for us, demonstrated by his suffering and sacrifice on the Cross, reminds me anew of the total surrender to our Lord that we are called to make. As Martin L. Smith wrote, "Is not the surrender of submission to an enemy, but the opposite, the laying down of our resistance to the One who loves me infinitely more than I can guess, the One who is more on my side than I am myself."

Secondly, the book emphasizes throughout (also like marriage) that Spiritual Maturity is a process in which we are not to expect perfection but learn to depend, increasingly, on the Holy Spirit to convict us of our sins, to lead us to repentance and forgiveness, and to empower us to grow.

For me, *Love Story* is further strengthened by what I know about Frank and Michelle Davis. Through the special friendship that my wife and I enjoy with the Davis family, I have seen up close that these Biblical truths about which he writes are also the core values by which he lives as a husband and father, as a follower of Christ, and as a faithful and passionate pastor and builder of disciples.

I am certain that many others will share my own gratitude to Frank Davis for writing this book, and I am confident that it will be a valuable resource for Christians of varying traditions seeking Biblically based helps for Spiritual Maturity.

H. Cobb "Cobby" Ware
Retired Presbyterian Pastor
(Over his forty years in ministry, H. Cobb Ware pastored three Presbyterian congregations and served with the Fellowship of Christian Athletes)

Chapter 1

The End of Religion

I grew up a religious kid in a religious family. Everyone in my family (my mom, my siblings, my grandparents, my cousins...everyone) believed in God, believed in Jesus, and even though many of us rarely read it, we believed in the Bible. On Sunday mornings, we went to church and while I enjoyed church most of the time, it wasn't as if I had a choice. My mom was amazing, but she was old school. She didn't give time outs for unruly children; she gave knockouts, and she did not negotiate with prepubescent terrorists. Mom said, "Go," so we went, and saying, "I'm not going," wasn't ever going be a pleasant experience. Church was an acquired taste, but we learned to like it.

We had an eclectic church experience. Technically, we were Catholics but my mom was raised AME and didn't really believe in denominations, so we did our fair share of hopping around. On any given Sunday, I could be in a folk mass, a soulful, gospel service, or some kind of weird hybrid. By the time I was in high school, we had a regular congregation, and we became pretty involved. I attended Sunday school in the mornings, was involved in the youth group, and even went on church retreats. One of my brothers and I played for the gospel choir, and we also played in a Christian band that did shows in churches all over the city, further expanding our range of diverse worship experiences. The more involved I became and the more experiences I had, the more I really came to appreciate worship in all of its myriad forms, but there was a downside to my exposure as well. Two things happened as I became more immersed in church culture: I began to see behind the curtain, and I became utterly disillusioned by the hypocrisy and shallowness of organized religion.

The first thing I did when I went away to college was to stop attending church. I still believed in God, but I just didn't see how attending was going to get me closer to Him. Besides, from my point of view, I had learned what I needed to learn. I had used my astonishing powers of discernment to pick out the best lessons from all the denominations I had visited and leave the useless stuff behind. In my mind, I was the most spiritual guy I knew. I wore a cross every day, was quick to defend Christianity in debates with my *less enlightened* friends, and I read the Bible a couple of times a year, with every intention of reading it more often. I had been baptized, gone through several other Catholic sacraments, and for good measure, had prayed Jesus into my heart when I was in junior high school and again a time or two in high school. I was a pretty moral dude. I wasn't one of those weird Jesus Freaks going door to door, but I was a good guy. I had dotted my religious i's and crossed my t's. I was fine; I was covered. There was just one problem. If I was honest, truly honest, I was miserable.

I was the good kid, the nice guy, the high achiever, but all of that was a *mask*, and by the end of my freshmen year of college, I was exhausted with the weight of wearing it. The real me was filled with anger and so much fear. Until I was eight years old, I grew up as part of the real-life version of the TV *Cosby* family. My dad was a doctor, my mom was an educator, we lived in upper middle-class Maryland suburbs, and all was perfect in my sitcom fantasy world. My parent's divorced when I was eight. After the divorce, my amazing mom raised four children by herself in Baltimore city. Baltimore is many things, but it will never be confused with being a suburb, and my life after that had a lot more in common with *Good Times* than the *Cosby Show*. We went through some incredibly tough times, but my mom, being the super hero that she was, kept it all together. My dad essentially disappeared from the scene. For the next twelve years after the divorce, I rarely ever spoke to him, and I only saw him a handful of times after he moved to California, sometime before my tenth birthday. I didn't understand it then, but it left something very broken inside me.

I hid it well, but since I was eight, anger and fear were my constant companions. They drove my accomplishments, sabotaged all my relationships, and fueled my growing sense of inadequacy, destroying me methodically, quietly from the inside out. I was everyone's friend but close to no one, a cocky and arrogant exterior with a terrified core, a chameleon who got along with everyone but himself. On a campus of 37,000 undergraduate students, I was lonely and broken, often wandering around late at night, wondering what was wrong with me.

I was a religious guy from a religious family, and it meant absolutely nothing. Religion couldn't help me; it couldn't console me; it couldn't make me whole. Religion couldn't heal the hurt, bitterness, and rejection that was growing inside me, devouring the best parts of me, like an alien monster yearning to break free. Religion is a lie. It is an empty promise that imprisons rather than empowers. It is a blind guide that leads its sheep to feast at a buffet featuring cheap grace, empty platitudes, and suffocating legalism, and leaves its guests stumbling off, drunk on pietistic pride. Religion confuses sacraments with salvation, clings to ritual instead of righteousness, and places sectarianism and denominationalism in the way of devotion. There is a reason why many of the most bitter, most judgmental, most miserable folks that you will ever meet are also among the most religious. Religion breaks hearts; it does not heal them. It causes wars; it does not end them. It leads people away from God, not toward Him. Religion is a lie. It could not help me because it simply has no power.

Now, I'm not suggesting that God is a lie or that faith in Him is futile. I believe that true religion, that fosters intimacy with the Almighty, has the power to totally transform lives. The brand of religion that I am referencing in this chapter is outside in spirituality instead of inside out, constantly consumed with the appearance of holiness rather than internal transformation. It is the type that evolves when conviction is buried under tradition and routine. Imagine falling in love and deciding to build a beautiful home for your loved one. Each day you work hard to add on additions to this beautiful dwelling to make it more remarkable until it becomes a stunning, sprawling mansion. The problem is that, along the way, you're working so hard expanding and taking care of the mansion that there is barely any contact with the one for whom you built it; the mansion has a life of its own and it has become the thing you serve. This analogy describes much of what has broken in modern Christianity. Religious tradition, ritual, sectarianism, systems, and structure while intended to serve God, in many cases have become a living, breathing monster that longs to be fed. Rather than being the place we come to find God, church has become an endless maze that makes it difficult to see Him, let alone connect with Him. To complicate matters further, in too many instances, faith is inherited instead of inspired, and the truth is that faith that is inherited is not faith at all. I experienced this emptiness in my youth.

Jesus is the answer, but He is not found in that kind of shallow spirituality. Jesus did not come to start a new religion. There were many creeds, dogmas, cults, and sects in Judea when He walked the earth. The last thing He came to do was to start a new one, called Christianity. No, Jesus did not come to start a new religion. He came for a totally different reason entirely. Jesus came to put an end to religion.

Through the days of Jesus's life, He showed us something better, truer than religion, nailing the old way to the cross and empowering a new path through the empty tomb. He offers relationship, not ritual, a vibrant, dynamic relationship with God through Christ. Just as Enoch walked with God, God wants to walk with you and me, and the door, the guide, the light, and the bridge to make that relationship a reality is Jesus.

It was during my sophomore year at the University of Maryland that God got my attention. I was dragged to a small Bible study group, and what I found changed my life. I found people filled with Christ's love that loved me and accepted me from day one. It was a life-giving group, part of a life-giving campus ministry, where Christianity wasn't just a religion; it was a true relationship with God. It was there that I first encountered the real Jesus and saw the power of personal discipleship and one- another love. I was saved shortly after making that connection, and over time, God moved my heart to go into the full-time ministry. Why? Because I was convinced that there were men and women just like me who were wandering around, angry, lost, and empty. Like me, they needed more than a church. They needed Jesus. I met my incredible wife, Michelle, in New York a few years after graduation, and together we've spent the last twenty-nine years as church planters and missionaries.

That small Bible study group saved my life and changed the entire course of it. What those brothers and sisters helped me to discover is exactly what this book, *Love Story*, strives to pass on to you. My goal is to assist you in using the scriptures to connect with God on a relational level. My prayer is that you will come to experience a Lord who loves you with unshakable passion and will learn not only how to love Him in return but how to let that love radiate throughout every aspect of your life.

The approach of *Love Story* is to use the analogy of the stages of a romantic relationship to transport readers on a journey of discovery that will ignite a personal rapport with the Creator. *Love Story* can help you fall in love with God for the first time, or for those who have a walk with Him, it is great way to strengthen and/or rekindle the bond that already exists. You also have the option of enhancing your experience by reading this book in conjunction with the *Love Story Workbook*. The workbook has helpful studies and videos that augment the information found in each chapter of *Love Story*.

Read on, embrace the *Love Story,* and let Jesus transform your mind and soul as you embark on the adventure of true discipleship. It is time to trade in religion for something more.

Chapter 2

Formal Introductions

Every great romance has a story, and every story has a beginning. A first meeting, the first date, the first kiss, each courtship has a series of firsts that spark the bond that changes both lives, forever. Whether the person with whom someone eventually falls in love is an individual that he/she has known for a while or a blind date, the movement from acquaintance, to like, to love is always a winding road that often involves an *Aha* moment. I remember mine.

I met my future wife, Michelle, in New York (she's a native New Yorker). We attended the same church and lived in the Bronx in the same neighborhood; in fact, her building was about one hundred feet from mine. Sometimes, we even waited at the same bus stop and caught the same bus on the way to work (more about that next chapter). Not only did we have many of the same friends, I was pretty close to one of her best friends and had been on dates with several ladies in Michelle's circle. I knew her; she knew me, on a superficial level, but we really hadn't truly met nor had a conversation longer than ten minutes. Most of what I knew about Michelle was what I had heard from other people; most of whom were telling me that I should take her out. Being stubborn, and slow to figure out what's good for me, it was a year before we actually went out on our first date. I don't remember all the details, but one thing I do remember is that it was on that date that I really saw her for the first time and realized that Michelle Griffith was someone that I desperately wanted to get to know better. That date was my first introduction to the true Michelle.

Building a relationship with Jesus is the same. Whether you come from a background where you know very little about Him or have known Him on some level your whole life, there needs to be a formal introduction, a time when we allow Jesus to show us clearly who He really is. So often, our view of Jesus is shaped by TV shows, movies, church, family, or our own imagination. It's not that these influences are bad. It's simply that a picture is painted; opinions are formed and sometimes calcified, purely on the words of others. Jesus is defined by everyone's words but His own. Before you read any further, take a deep breath, erase your preconceptions, and resolve not to blindly accept anyone's testimony about Him...including mine.

To quote my brother, Scott, "It's time to do your own research."

If you're willing to do that, you'll find that Jesus is quite capable of speaking for Himself. He makes some rather shocking and remarkable claims, and provides a test by which we can verify whether they are true. In this chapter, we are going to examine some key scriptures about Him. For these passages and all others presented in this book, I strongly encourage you to read far more than the excerpts that I present. I suggest that you read the chapters before and after so that you can understand the full context.

Jesus Is the One

John 14:6

⁶ Jesus answered, "I am the way and the truth and the life. No one comes to the Father except through me.

Who does Jesus say He is? One of the principle claims that Jesus makes about Himself is that He is the One. He makes this assertion here in John 14:6 and elsewhere. It is a bold declaration and the type of claim that divides a room; it does not tend to unify it. He does not allow us to write Him off as just another holy man or just another prophet. According to this statement, His teachings are not just one of many ways to reach enlightenment; He is the *only path*, the *only way*. This is a radical claim. If it is false, Jesus is a raving lunatic, who should be ignored, not worshipped. If it is true, well, it changes everything. The two passages below will help gain some insight into this assertion and its basis.

John 1:1-5

In the beginning was the Word, and the Word was with God, and the Word was God. ² He was with God in the beginning. ³ Through him all things were made; without him nothing was made that has been made. ⁴ In him was life, and that life was the light of all mankind. ⁵ The light shines in the darkness, and the darkness has not overcome it.

John 1:14

¹⁴ The Word became flesh and made his dwelling among us. We have seen his glory, the glory of the one and only Son, who came from the Father, full of grace and truth.

These two passages can build your faith or break your brain. For me, it does a little of both. John 1:1 states, *In the beginning was the Word and Word was with God.* OK, that seems straightforward but it continues, *And the Word was God.* Huh? Verse 14 informs us that this eternal Word became flesh and lived among us. OK. So, the Bible is saying that the Word is Jesus, and Jesus left heaven and lived as a man here on earth. It is also saying that Jesus (the Word) was with God in the beginning and is God. What? Does your brain hurt yet? How can Jesus be God and yet be separate from Him? How can He both be God and be God's son? From my limited human perspective, this is impossible. My Friend Bob cannot be Joe's son and also be Joe. They cannot be both one and separate. Yet, this is the claim of the Bible, and it makes it in several places and even alludes to this reality in the first chapter of the Bible's first book.

Genesis 1:26

²⁶ Then God said, "Let us make mankind in our image, in our likeness, so that they may rule over the fish in the sea and the birds in the sky, over the livestock and all the wild animals, and over all the creatures that move along the ground."

God said, *"Let us make mankind."* Who is this *us*? I believe He is talking to Jesus (The Word), the one who is next to Him, the one who was with Him since the beginning, the one through whom He made the universe (Hebrews 1:2), the one who is separate from Him, the one who is a part of Him. Jesus is God and He is separate, one with God but also apart. Two things can be true at once; we can accept the impossibility of this and still accept that it is true. Why? The truth is if there is a supreme being, His fingerprint is the existence of unimaginable truth.

For God to be God everything about Him is inconceivable; everything goes beyond not only human experience but outside the boundaries of human imagination. If God truly exits, if there really is an omnipotent, omniscient, omnipresent being that existed before existence and spoke everything into reality, how could it be any other way? He can hear my prayers, your prayers, and prayers from all around the world at once. He can be on the throne of heaven, in your home, and inside you simultaneously. He is the whisper before the big bang and the something that existed in endless nothingness. If God exists, He is not subject to the laws of nature, to the concepts of time, or space. He created them. He is not subject to the computer program that is our reality. He wrote the program, built the computer, and dwells outside of it, even while He is ubiquitous inside of it. He is God, and I am not. I cannot make Him less than who He is by attempting to restrict His capabilities to the confines of what I can explain. I am an ant trying to grasp the wonders of the universe, and the fact that Jesus is both God and God's son is one of those wonders.

I don't believe that anyone can truly understand how the relationship between Jesus and God works, but I can share the best analogy I've heard. Let me caution that while this might be helpful, it still falls short. In this analogy, God is the ocean. If you think of God as the ocean and you took a cup of the ocean and boiled it, that steam would be the Holy Spirit. It would have all the qualities of God but in a different form. If you took a cup of God and froze it, the ice would be Jesus and if you threw those frozen cubes to the shore, it would symbolize Jesus coming to earth. The cubes would have all the qualities of the ocean in a different form, separate from the ocean but the same. So it is with Jesus and God.

In my opinion, the most intriguing question concerning John 1:1-14 is why John would start his gospel this way. Why start his gospel with a cosmic brain twister too big for us to understand? I believe that John had two important objectives. He wanted to establish the divinity of Jesus, and He desired to illustrate the aspect of God that Jesus is. Jesus is the Word. He is the living breathing Word of God, and during His time on earth, the very Word of God became flesh. Therefore, if this is the case, this has some implications and raises some challenging questions. For me, two questions immediately stand out. Is it possible to have a relationship with Jesus without having a relationship with God's word? Is it possible to walk with Jesus without holding tightly to the word of God?

I believe that the Bible isn't *just* a book. I believe that it is the inspired word of God. So, if Jesus is the Word, the scriptures are literally a part of Him, the part of Him that He has revealed to the world. He will speak to us, guide us, and reveal Himself to us through the words on its pages. Prayer is how we talk to Jesus, but the scriptures are the primary way that He talks to us. Praying without searching the scriptures is like being engaged in a conversation where one person does a bunch of talking, doesn't give the other person the opportunity to speak, and then has the audacity to end the chat with, "Good talk. Let's do this again, soon." Jesus wants to be involved in the conversation. He doesn't want just to hear my prayers; He has a few things, more than a few things, to say to me. The scriptures are the most

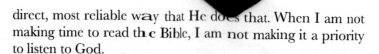

direct, most reliable way that He does that. When I am not making time to read the Bible, I am not making it a priority to listen to God.

Why was I so empty for so long? Partly, because I thought that going to church and having good intentions equated to living a Godly life and that relying on the bits and pieces of spiritual knowledge I gleamed from church, my family, and my own reasoning was all I needed to find my way. I figured that as long as I knew the big picture things about Jesus, it wasn't necessary to know or worry about the details. Reading the Bible was a luxury not a necessity. To me, it was like a manual for a bike or a TV or something. Well, I've never read a manual in my life (yes, I'm sorry to say that I'm that guy). I generally skim them, get the gist, and get other people to fill in anything I need to know. I mean, who has time to read a manual? To me, the scriptures were like a recipe from a cookbook and, in my mind, as long as I had the key ingredients (belief in God and Jesus, following the Ten Commandments or at least the realistic ones, being a good person, etc.), it didn't really matter what else I left out or added. I was going to be OK. This approach not only explains much of what was wrong with me spiritually but also why I was such a bad cook. I was sadly mistaken about the scriptures. Following Jesus is not about finding and following the right spiritual recipe; it is about forging a relationship, and healthy relationships cannot be formed by trying to discover the minimum requirements. The foundation of any beneficial relationship is spending time together. The Bible is the key to accomplishing this.

It's not just any book. It's not just words on a page. There is power in these pages. Hebrews 4:12 states that the Bible is living and active; the words in this book are a piece of the Word Himself and the scriptures are as alive and dynamic as He is. II Timothy 3:16 shares that the Bible is both God breathed and useful, able to teach us, correct us, and chastise us and goes on to explain that it can train us in how to be righteous, making the Bible the original life coach. Psalm 119:9 teaches that the word is the way to keep our path pure. Hebrews 4:12 reveals that the scriptures are the key to internal transformation, having the power to divide soul and spirit and to judge the thoughts and attitudes of the heart. Ephesians 6:17 echoes this sentiment, instructing us that the sword of the spirit is the word of God.

The word is the Holy Spirit's weapon of choice, for convicting me, comforting me, protecting me, and transforming me. The Bible makes these claims about itself and many more. How is it able to accomplish all of this? Because it is not merely a book that teaches us cool spiritual principles; it is the vehicle by which we walk with Jesus, and everyone who walks with Jesus will be changed.

Jesus is the Word. I cannot draw close to Him without clinging to the part of Him He left for me to hold on to. I was trying to experience Him with a closed Bible, trying to have a daily walk with Him without having daily time in His word. I was chasing a mirage, a Jesus of myth and tradition, while Jesus Himself was sitting on my bookshelf collecting dust, dying to converse with me. Even when I was attending church once a week or more, my time there was never going to be a substitute for spending daily time in prayer and scripture. If I had understood that it was about developing a relationship rather than paying my spiritual dues, this would have been obvious to me. Relationships demand time, intimacy, and daily devotion. Any man who is married or has a serious relationship knows that spending public time with your significant other isn't the same as spending quality time together. If I take my wife to the movies, we have dinner with a group of friends, go home, and spend time with the kids together, and I don't have any private interplay with the Mrs., I'm being very foolish to think that all of that interaction means we've spent quality time together. Trust me, if I don't arrange for some alone time for the two of us to connect, I'm going to hear the most dreaded four words in the English language, "WE

NEED TO TALK." Going to the movies, hanging with friends and the kids, this is important stuff, but it's not a substitute for one on one intimacy.

It's the same with Jesus. Going to church or a small group is a good thing, and it meets an important need in its own right (one we'll talk more about in chapter eight), but it cannot be a substitute for spending intimate time with Jesus. I had gone to church my whole life and had no clue who Jesus really was. Why? I had never invested in getting to know Him, one on one, talking to Him through my prayer, and allowing Him to speak to me, guide me, through His word. When we decide to invest in this daily intimacy, we will have our formal introduction to Jesus.

The Bible claims that Jesus is the one. My suggestion is to open the Bible, walk with Him yourself, and judge for yourself if this is just another book and if Jesus is just another man.

He Can Prove It

John 7:16-17

16 Jesus answered, "My teaching is not my own. It comes from the one who sent me. 17 Anyone who chooses to do the will of God will find out whether my teaching comes from God or whether I speak on my own.

Every family has defining characteristics. Growing up, our family had two: a love of music and a passion for arguing. We would argue about anything, anywhere, anytime. My mom wanted us to think for ourselves, be confident, and to learn to articulate our views clearly, so she encouraged us to develop our own opinions about life, but we had to be able to defend them. To survive in the Davis household, you had to be quick witted, and you had to have thick skin. Sometimes…most of the time, the dueling opinions would get a little crazy and go way too far. How bad was it? The first time Michelle spent time around my family, she pulled me aside and asked, "What is wrong with you people?" We could be a little intense.

I loved to argue. On campus, I would debate anyone and everyone. I would make a case against abortion, and just when my opponent was stammering and swaying, I'd switch sides and argue for it. When I had him persuaded again, I'd switch sides again. Befuddled, they'd ask, "Which side do you believe in?" My reply, "I believe in winning." I learned early on that a persuasive person could make an effective case for just about anything and could make a lie sound better than the truth. Now, you may be wondering what any of this has to do with John 7:16-17. I'm glad you asked.

Jesus says that He is the one, but He's not the only one making that claim. He says that He is the way, but there is no limit to the myriad alternate paths laid before us. Why Jesus? Why not some other way? A good argument can be made for different religions or no religion at all. A compelling case can be made for just about anything, and the tide of contemporary morality is always shifting and changing. If anyone is trying to set his/her moral compass based on the majority, good luck. Not only is the morality of the masses constantly in flux, it is not anchored to a standard, following whatever chorus of people shout the loudest. If enough people say something loudly enough and long enough, it becomes canon. So, should I follow whoever is winning the argument? How can I know which way to go?

Is sex before marriage a sin or is that belief simply archaic and unrealistic? Is marriage the cornerstone of civilization or a cultural invention that goes against biology and has outlived its usefulness? Is homosexuality a sin, a biological imperative, or the sacred right of people to love whomever they choose? Is Chicago pizza really better than New York pizza? There are so many questions. How can we know which way to choose?

Jesus has an answer. In John 7:16-17, He says that He is the one, His way is the only way, and He can prove it. We don't have to take His word for it. What is His proof? He says that if we follow His words, we will be able to tell for ourselves whether they come from man or from God. Read them and obey them, and you will see. His way works. It works in the short run and in the long run. His way works and others don't.

The world is falling apart and all of its wisdom and philosophies are speeding up the process, not holding it together. Marriages are crumbling in divorce; lives are sinking in the quicksand of depression; families are drowning in a sea of addiction: addiction to sex, illegal drugs, legal drugs…take your pick. There is no magic in conventional wisdom. We've looked behind the curtain, and the wizard of our best thinking has been exposed as a fraud. My life was in shambles, and none of my ideas, no matter how persuasive, could put it back together. My way didn't work. Jesus does.

Jesus proposes a simple test, a scientific test. Put aside all preconceptions and tradition, read His word with an open mind and heart, and see if it doesn't touch you like nothing else. Walk with Him, the Word, and see if He doesn't change you in ways that nothing else ever has. Anyone can win a debate, can fight for a cause, or start a *holy* war. The goal is to win at life. Isn't it worth finding out if Jesus is the key to accomplishing this? Jesus invites us to follow Him, try Him on, and do your own research.

Belief Is Not Enough

John 8:31-32

31 To the Jews who had believed him, Jesus said, "If you hold to my teaching, you are really my disciples. 32 Then you will know the truth, and the truth will set you free."

In the above passage, Jesus is speaking to a group of Jews who believed in His teachings (most Jews did not) and instructs them that simply believing is not enough. Belief is the first step but holding to His teachings is the key.

According to Jesus, holding to His teachings leads to discipleship, discipleship allows us to know the truth, and the truth will set us free from sin. This passage runs contrary to what I grew up believing and what I heard in most of the churches I attended. I was under the impression that simply believing was enough and that as long as I acknowledged that Jesus was the Christ and desired to be saved that I was in good shape spiritually. In my mind, that was the beauty of grace, a whole lot of blessing with little to no effort. My view of being saved was closer to witchcraft than a Biblical model. Say a magic prayer, believe the words, and poof, everything is better. Sounds good, but it's just not representative of Jesus's teachings.

Not only does John 8:31-32 teach that there is more to it than just belief; this concept is supported by many other passages. James 2:17 teaches us that faith by itself if not accompanied by action is dead. James 2:26 tells us that faith without deeds is as dead as a body without the spirit.

James 2:19

You believe that there is one God. Good! Even the demons believe that—and shudder.

Are you sensing a theme? Obviously, if I had been a student of the Bible, I would have realized the error in my theology, but I also would have realized it if I had treated being a Christian as a relationship with Jesus rather than as religion.

Once I understood that this is relational, this became very simple. There is no relationship where belief is enough. I'm married to an amazing wife. Twenty-nine years ago, Michelle and I stood in front of a church in Manhattan, full of people, and pledged devotion by reciting incredible vows. I vowed to love my wife, be faithful to her, etc. So, if later on my wife had caught me cheating (It's OK, baby. This is just a fictitious example) and confronted me saying, "How could you do this? What about our vows?" How would she feel if I replied, "Everything's fine, honey, I still believe in our vows. I'm just not holding to them." Would she be OK with that? Of course not, she would now be part of the prison ministry, and I would be swimming with the fishes in the Hudson River.

What about seatbelts? If I believe in seatbelts but don't wear them and get in an accident, going one hundred miles an hour, do you think my belief in seat belts will save me? No, I will fly through that windshield like superman. In the same way, faith without obedience is useless.

So, what does it mean to hold to His word? Is Jesus teaching that we have to be perfect to be His disciples? No, but we have to have a standard and make every effort to hold on to it. The truth is we all do have standards for our lives; it is just that in most cases our standard is not the Bible. For most people, our morality and behavior is determined by feelings, circumstances, opinions, and traditions. Feelings are a big one. If we feel happy, we're nice. If we feel angry, we lash out or get bitter. If we feel amorous, we...you get it. Discipleship involves clinging to the Bible as the standard of our behavior, regardless of our feelings, circumstances, traditions, and opinions. So, if my wife makes me mad, my commitment is to respond according to Jesus's wishes instead of my emotions. I give my best effort to follow His way, and when I blow it, I get up and follow the scriptures instructions on how to own my shortcomings and bounce back.

This is the practice of obedience, but the power of obedience is that it is a method of walking with Jesus. As we walk with Him, He empowers us to obey and reveals His truth to us, peeling back the layers of meaning of His words like an onion and helping the message to travel from our heads to our hearts. I can read the Bible everyday and get nothing out of it other than some answers for Bible trivia. The Bible cannot be truly understood until we walk with Jesus through daily obedience. This is the walk of a disciple. Then we will know the truth, and the truth will set us free.

Why was I so miserable? I wasn't free, and my belief was not enough to get me there.

A Test Is Coming

John 12:47-48

⁴⁷ "If anyone hears my words but does not keep them, I do not judge that person. For I did not come to judge the world, but to save the world. ⁴⁸ There is a judge for the one who rejects me and does not accept my words; the very words I have spoken will condemn them at the last day.

This is a good news, bad news, good news passage. The good news is that Jesus did not come to earth 2,000 years ago to judge the world. He came to save it. The *bad* news is that there is a judge. Who or what is the judge? Verse 48 tells us that Jesus's very words will be the thing that judges us on the last day. There are other scriptures that reference Jesus returning to judge the world and still others that refer to God as the judge. Is this a contradiction? Of course not, remember, Jesus is the Word and the Word is God. Jesus is not saying in this passage that He is not coming back to judge the world. He is sharing exactly the mechanism He is using for administering His rulings. We are each going to be judged by the teachings He left behind for us, and where do we find these teachings? The Bible.

This is either the best news in the world or the scariest. If we are holding to the scriptures and walking with Jesus, this passage should give us tremendous confidence, but if you are like I was, and your Bible is a paperweight and a place for family genealogies, this is a problem, a very big problem.

Imagine if you had a college course and the professor instructed you on the first day of class that your whole grade was going to be your final exam. That's some serious pressure, right? But there's good news. He's going to give you all the questions for the final today, and you have the whole semester to study. That's good, right? It gets better.

He's also going to give you the answers, and you have the answers to study all semester as well. OK, now we're getting somewhere. He then informs you that He is making himself available, morning, noon, and night to consult for help, and to top it off he's going to assign to anyone interested a personal teaching assistant that will follow the student around, supplying 24-hour personal tutoring, encouragement, and life-coaching. That's a sweet deal, an easy A, right? So, if a student goofed around all semester, didn't seek help, forgot to study, and ended up failing, whose fault would it be? This is exactly what Jesus is saying about His words. Every question about life and godliness is found in the Bible, and every answer about those topics is found in its passages. In addition, He himself will walk with us and guide us, encourage, and strengthen us if we let him. So, on judgment day, if we are clinging to empty religion or useless traditions or our own opinions rather than walking confidently in a relationship with Jesus, who do we have to blame? What possible good reason would we have for putting ourselves in this situation?

The bad news is that the ultimate test is coming, and it is unavoidable. The good news is that Jesus has set us up to win. The other good news is that even though life gives us a whole lot of tests and trials along the way, His word has the power to help us be victorious through these obstacles as well. Everyone is going to run the gauntlet of hurt, loss, failure, regret, sin, and guilt. We all face Goliaths bigger and stronger than us along the way. Well, here's a secret. We weren't meant to face Goliath alone. Walk with Jesus, depend on His word, and you will have a partner bigger than any giant you will ever face.

Here's the best news. God wants to take the insecurity and guess work out of our relationship with Him, and He's supplied a more reliable metric for determining how we are doing spiritually than ourselves. That's good because no one lies to me more than I do. One of the first lessons I learned as a young married man was how to answer the question, "How's the marriage going?" Early on, when someone would ask us the question, I'd be quick to answer, "Oh, it's going great. We're doing fine." Then they'd turn to my wife for her response and she'd start crying. She wasn't fine, and if she wasn't fine, we certainly weren't fine. I was just clueless and self-deceived (don't judge me). I learned to answer the question better. When asked, I now turn and ask Michelle, 'Honey, how are we doing?" Spiritually, it was much the same. For too long, I was asking myself the question, "Frank, how are you doing spiritually?" And I would answer, "Great." Like my marriage, I didn't realize that I was in no position to answer the question. I lacked and still lack the proper perspective. I needed to let Jesus answer that question for me, understanding that I couldn't be doing well if we weren't doing well together. When I started devoting myself to the study of scripture, I started listening to Jesus's evaluation of my spiritual health and decided to let Him be my standard rather than having a standard of my own invention. Even though I value my multitude of brilliant opinions, God is not impressed. He's not going to ask for my advice on Judgment Day. I had to ask myself the question, "If the Bible is going to be the book that judges me, shouldn't it be my standard for life?" Deciding to let it be that for me is one of the most significant decisions I have ever made.

So, if Jesus is the one, and the word is both the way we walk with Him and the standard by which we are going to be judged, what does that mean for you? As I see it, if you are reading this book, you are in one of three categories. The first option is that you are unsure about the Bible and its claims and not totally convinced that Jesus is who He and others say He is. The second option is that you are someone who believes but has never really made the time to be a student of the word and never understood its importance in having a relationship with Christ. Or lastly, you are someone who is well aware of all this and has already made the commitment to walk with Jesus daily, through the word.

No matter what your circumstance, I want to give you a challenge.

For the next three weeks, I challenge you to make the decision to walk with the Word daily, and see if it makes a major difference in your life. This involves reading the Bible everyday but it is more than that. Don't just read the Bible like it is a novel or a history book. My encouragement is to treat it as part of a conversation with Jesus where you make time to pray to Him and look to the scriptures for the message He is speaking to you.

The question you might be thinking is, "Where should I start?" Start with one of the four gospels. I normally, suggest John, but any gospel (Matthew, Mark or Luke) will be fine. Why the gospels? Ultimately, the Bible is Jesus's story. The gospels chronicle His time on earth and give us the most direct understanding of His life and His character. In my opinion, the better someone understands the Jesus of the gospels, the easier it is to see Him in the rest of the scriptures and to understand why events, particularly Old Testament events, had to transpire the way they did. So, start with John or one of the other gospels. Put the emphasis on understanding and applying, quality over quantity. It doesn't help to read ten chapters if there is limited retention and little to no practical application. Make a three-week commitment and at the end of the three weeks, see where you are. If you are someone who has your doubts about Jesus, this is an opportunity to put Him to the test. If you are a believer but Bible novice, this is an opportunity to take your first step from religion to relationship. If you are a seasoned disciple, this is a chance to recommit to the basics. No matter where you are in your spiritual walk, you can benefit from your formal introduction.

Chapter 3

The Love Letter

Sometimes in the movies, two people gaze at each other from across the room and connect, instantly falling in love. Okay, that makes for a cool scene, but in my experience, that's not how it normally works. One of the differences between romantic comedies and real life is that in the real world two people rarely feel the same thing at the same time. More often than not, one party catches the love bug before the other. From that point, dog chases cat or cat chases dog until the other party catches the love virus as well or is fed up and runs the pursuer off. In my single days, I experienced all aspects of this scenario. I've been the one who chased, I've been the one who was chased away, and believe it or not, I've been the one who was pursued.

I mentioned earlier how Michelle and I knew each other for a year before we went on our first date. We went to the same church, lived in the same neighborhood, and even occasionally waited at the bus stop together and caught the same bus on our way to work. What I didn't share and didn't know until after we got married was that she worked later than I. She found out what time I caught the bus and would wake up early so that we would be out there together. You see, though I was clueless, Michelle had a crush on me first, and catching the bus together was part of her well-crafted, diabolical plan to rope me in. So, even though I thought it was my idea to eventually ask her out, I was just succumbing to her powerful Jedi mind trick. Our roles would eventually flip after I hurt her feelings months later (it wasn't my fault...really), but it's been a matter of some pride that I can boast that, initially, Michelle was pursuing me.

When I started studying the Bible, I realized that Michelle wasn't the first person to go to great lengths in order to establish a relationship with me. In fact, someone had been madly in love with me and had worked hard throughout my life to try to get my attention. God was my pursuer, and he's yours as well. He loved us first. Before we were fully formed, before we cared about Him, knew who He was, or even knew much about ourselves, God was dreaming, planning, and fighting for a relationship with each one of us. Growing up in church, I'd heard that God loved me my entire life. I guess, I accepted that as truth, but it wasn't something that affected my everyday life. It was more like a random fact than a life altering revelation. It wasn't until I really understood the cross and what it meant that I began to understand the depth of God's love for me and that His passion for me demanded a personal response.

Imagine being back in high school and hearing rumors that some random girl or guy you had never met had feelings for you. OK, that's interesting, but for most of us, that's where it would stop. Now, suppose one day that someone gives you a letter from your admirer. This letter is painstakingly written by this person, with obvious time and care. In it is outlined how passionately this individual feels for you and the depths to which he/she would go to show the full measure of their love. Now, whether you consider this gesture romantic or more than a little stalky, I have to believe it would definitely get your full attention. The letter would not be some random fact or a footnote to your day. Whether it excites you, terrifies you, sweeps you off your feet, or makes you want to call 911, my guess is that it would invoke a powerful response. In fact, such an act of love demands a response, one way or another.

The cross is Jesus's love letter, written with His blood, with pain and tears, by His own hand. I do not believe that anyone can have any inkling of Jesus's love for him without understanding the cross, and it is impossible to truly understand the cross and its significance and not have a strong reaction. Not everyone who grasps Jesus's love letter is going to decide to follow Him, but it will invoke an emotional response and leave a life altering impression, one way or another.

Acts 2:36-37

36 *"Therefore let all Israel be assured of this: God has made this Jesus, whom you crucified, both Lord and Messiah."*

37 *When the people heard this, they were cut to the heart and said to Peter and the other apostles, "Brothers, what shall we do?"*

Acts 2:40-41

40 *With many other words he warned them; and he pleaded with them, "Save yourselves from this corrupt generation."*

41 *Those who accepted his message were baptized, and about three thousand were added to their number that day.*

In the above passages, Peter is speaking to a large crowd on the day of Pentecost, approximately seven weeks after Jesus's death. He spoke to the crowd about Jesus with words that are recorded in Acts 2 and, according to verse 40, with many other words that are not recorded. His message was primarily about Jesus's life, His death on the cross, and His resurrection. Many of the members of the crowd were so moved, cut to the heart so deeply that, they turned themselves in, begging the apostles to let them know what they could do to set things right. Learning the answer, three thousand of the individuals who heard this sermon were baptized that day. This is truly amazing. But do you know the question that intrigues me? Why was their response to the message of the cross so different from what mine had been for so long? These people heard that Jesus, the Messiah, died for them and because of them and it moved them to the point that the knowledge transformed their lives. I had heard the same message virtually every Sunday of my life, and it barely caused me to raise an eyebrow. It's clear that there was a big disconnect. It was personal for them and just Sunday school knowledge for me. They understood something that I clearly missed and my relationship with God never really took off until I found it. What I've learned is that hearing the message of the cross with your head or letting the love letter stir your heart is the difference between being religious or falling in love with Jesus.

Part of the problem that kept me trapped in religion for so many years, was that I was looking at Jesus through a filter that prevented the true impact of the cross from registering, a filter that the crowd in Acts 2 did not have. There are a couple of truths that I've learned since that have helped me and others remove that filter, and one of the keys was really connecting with Jesus's suffering. Jesus suffered emotionally, physically, and spiritually in ways and for reasons that are important to understand. Let's talk a little bit about His emotional suffering.

Jesus Suffered Emotionally

This obvious truth, that Jesus suffered emotionally, was the source of much of my disconnect. In part, it was because the cross for me was an image seen on church buildings, t-shirts, and bumper stickers. Unlike the crowd in Acts 2, I had never personally seen its horror and the emotional trauma it caused. The other aspect was that for me Jesus was not a real person. I believed in Him, but the version of Him I had created in my mind was so holy, so spiritual, and so divine, it was impossible for me to picture him having emotions like you and me. Yet, the mystery of Jesus is that He is both fully divine and fully human. That means He felt everything that I would have felt if I were to undergo the same ordeal. What exactly did Jesus feel?

Matthew 26:36-44

36 Then Jesus went with his disciples to a place called Gethsemane, and he said to them, "Sit here while I go over there and pray." 37 He took Peter and the two sons of Zebedee along with him, and he began to be sorrowful and troubled. 38 Then he said to them, "My soul is overwhelmed with sorrow to the point of death. Stay here and keep watch with me."

39 Going a little farther, he fell with his face to the ground and prayed, "My Father, if it is possible, may this cup be taken from me. Yet not as I will, but as you will."

40 Then he returned to his disciples and found them sleeping. "Couldn't you men keep watch with me for one hour?" he asked Peter. 41 "Watch and pray so that you will not fall into temptation. The spirit is willing, but the flesh is weak."

42 He went away a second time and prayed, "My Father, if it is not possible for this cup to be taken away unless I drink it, may your will be done."

43 When he came back, he again found them sleeping, because their eyes were heavy. 44 So he left them and went away once more and prayed the third time, saying the same thing.

Luke 22:39-44

39 Jesus went out as usual to the Mount of Olives, and his disciples followed him. 40 On reaching the place, he said to them, "Pray that you will not fall into temptation." 41 He withdrew about a stone's throw beyond them, knelt down and prayed, 42 "Father, if you are willing, take this cup from me; yet not my will, but yours be done." 43 An angel from heaven appeared to him and strengthened him. 44 And being in anguish, he prayed more earnestly, and his sweat was like drops of blood falling to the ground.

Crucifixion was a slow, incredibly painful method of execution, reserved for the most reviled members of society. As a carpenter's son, as a resident of Palestine, Jesus had almost certainly witnessed this act and understood the agony and humiliation associated with it, and in His actions in Gethsemane, we witness the intersection of that knowledge and His humanity. He knew what was before him, that He was going to be crucified, and He felt emotionally what most of us would have felt in that circumstance. He was completely overwhelmed, overwhelmed to the point of death, and spent, the evening praying and even attempted to get three of His closest friends, John, James, and Peter to pray with him. They could not keep their eyes open, leaving Jesus to face this emotional dilemma by himself. How do you think that made him feel? Jesus continued to pray, so emotional that He fell face down and according to Luke 22, His sweat fell to the ground like drops of blood. And what did He ask? He begged God to take this away, to find some other way. He wanted out. Yet, because of Jesus's incredible love for His father and for us, He added not my will but yours. In other words, if there is any other way for your will to be done, God, please, let's do plan B, but at the end of the day, if this is what it takes, I'll go through with it. Jesus prayed this prayer, distraught and in turmoil, three times.

Matthew 26:47-50

47 While he was still speaking, Judas, one of the Twelve, arrived. With him was a large crowd armed with swords and clubs, sent from the chief priests and the elders of the people. 48Now the betrayer had arranged a signal with them: "The one I kiss is the man; arrest him."49Going at once to Jesus, Judas said, "Greetings, Rabbi!" and kissed him.

50 Jesus replied, "Do what you came for, friend."

Then the men stepped forward, seized Jesus and arrested him.

Shortly after completing His prayer, Jesus was arrested, having been betrayed by Judas, who was hired by Jesus's enemies to determine a secluded place to apprehend Jesus at night and to identify Him. Why was that necessary? The nighttime arrest was important because there was fear of arresting Jesus during the day because He was adored by the crowds, and His enemies feared a riot. The purpose of having an individual identify him is that before the dawn of Facebook, selfies, TV, wanted posters, and the printing press, having an individual make an actual in person I.D. was the only way to confirm that the right man was being captured.

It had to be extremely painful for Jesus that Judas was the one who betrayed him. Judas was on of Jesus's twelve handpicked apostles, who had spent most of the previous three years traveling with Jesus, walking where He walked, serving where He served, and preaching where He preached. Not only did they do ministry together, they did life together, making Judas one of Jesus's closest friends. So how would you feel if a family member or one of your closest friends betrayed you with a kiss? Even if you knew it was coming, would that make it hurt less or more? When I read verse fifty, I can almost feel Jesus's pain, and feel His heart breaking. This was just part of the emotional torture Jesus endured.

Take the time to read the remainder of the crucifixion account from Matthew 26:51 to Matthew 27:56 and in those verses, you'll see more of Christ's journey. All of Jesus's followers fled and deserted Him, He was arrested and dragged before the chief priests and the Sanhedrin, His close friend, Peter denied Jesus three times, false witnesses told lies about Him, and throughout the ordeal, He was spat upon, slapped, ridiculed, and taunted. How would you feel? How tough would that be for you? If you can answer that question, you can begin to understand the emotional suffering of Jesus.

Jesus Suffered Physically

When Jesus was before the Sanhedrin, He was blindfolded, punched, slapped, and spit upon. All of this was painful, both physically and emotionally. The fact that Jesus was slapped has always stood out to me. If you've ever been slapped, (I have…and yes, I deserved it), you know that the physical sting is amplified by the sheer humiliation. Now, all of this was painful, but Jesus's ordeal greatly intensified after He was brought before Pilate and designated to be flogged and crucified.

Matthew 27:26-31

26 Then he released Barabbas to them. But he had Jesus flogged, and handed him over to be crucified.

27 Then the governor's soldiers took Jesus into the Praetorium and gathered the whole company of soldiers around him. 28 They stripped him and put a scarlet robe on him, 29 and then twisted together a crown of thorns and set it on his head. They put a staff in his right hand. Then they knelt in front of him and mocked him. "Hail, king of the Jews!" they said. 30 They spit on him, and took the staff and struck him on the head again and again. 31 After they had mocked him, they took off the robe and put his own clothes on him. Then they led him away to crucify him.

Verse 26 lets us know that Jesus was flogged. Flogging and the other horrific abuse that Jesus endured are events that fall outside of modern day experience, and even movie recreations do not do justice to the scope of the brutality. Much of the information that I will share in my effort to express His torment is pulled from three articles: *A Physicians View of the Crucifixion of Jesus Christ* written by Dr. C. Truman Davis, a medical doctor, and articles by Mark Driscoll and Dr. Douglass Jacoby on the same topic.

In keeping with the first century practice of flogging, Jesus was stripped of His clothing, His hands were tied over His head, and He was whipped on His shoulders, back, buttocks, and legs with a flagellum. The flagellum consisted of several short leather thongs with balls of iron or lead attached to the ends. The device was used for scourging and generally left the victim near the point of death. It was so extreme and debasing a form of torture, that, like crucifixion, Roman citizens were exempt from it. Many preachers have said that Jesus received thirty-nine lashes, in keeping with Jewish law, but this simply was not the case. Jesus was flogged by Romans and the duration of His punishment was subject to the whim of His tormentors. Dr. C. Truman Davis uses the following words to describe what transpired during Jesus' scourging.

At first, the heavy thongs cut through the skin only. Then, as the blows continue, they cut deeper into subcutaneous tissues, producing first an oozing of blood from the capillaries and veins of the skin, and finally spurting arterial bleeding from vessels in the underlying muscles. The small balls of lead first produce large, deep bruises, which are broken open by subsequent blows.

Finally, the skin of the back is hanging in long ribbons and the entire area is an unrecognizable mass of torn, bleeding tissue. When it is determined by the centurion in charge that the prisoner is near death, the beating is stopped.

After the beating stopped, with no time to recover, Jesus was taken to the Praetorium where He was subjected to further abuse and ridicule. The centurions placed a crown of thorns on His head, the thorns tearing into His scalp as they did, put a purple robe on Him, and mocked Him. After they became tired of this, they took a rod and struck Him on His head again and again. How severe was this beating?

Isaiah 52:13-15

See, my servant will act wisely
he will be raised and lifted up and highly exalted.
14 Just as there were many who were appalled at him
his appearance was so disfigured beyond that of any human being
and his form marred beyond human likeness—
15 so he will sprinkle many nations,
and kings will shut their mouths because of him.
For what they were not told, they will see,
and what they have not heard, they will understand.

In prophesying about the suffering of the coming Messiah, approximately seven hundred fifty years before Jesus's birth, Isaiah wrote that the Messiah's appearance would be disfigured and His face marred beyond human likeness. In other words, Christ was so badly beaten that He could barely be recognized as being human. Imagine if someone took a police baton and struck a loved one in the head repeatedly. Imagine the pain. Visualize the damage it would cause. This is what happened to Jesus. After this, they removed the purple robe. Now if you've ever had a cut and put a cloth on it to stop the bleeding, you know how much it hurts to rip it off after the blood coagulates and the cloth sticks to the wound. Remember Jesus' back. Remember how it was torn, with skin hanging in bloody strips. The robe had inevitably clung to the wounds as the blood dried. It had to be ripped off causing even more pain and suffering. This is hard for me to imagine and even harder for me to process, but the worst part is that all of this was just appetizer for the suffering Jesus would endure during crucifixion.

With crucifixion, the upright portion of the cross (or stipes) stayed fixed to the ground at the site of execution. The cross arm (or patibulum), weighing roughly 110 pounds, was normally placed on the back of the victim and he was forced to carry it to the location of his crucifixion. In Jesus's case, when it was clear that He was unable to carry the cross arm, a man named Simon of Cyrene was forced to carry it in His place. Once at the location, Jesus was thrown down on His back with His arms outstretched along the crossbar and nails were driven into His wrists.

Nails, approximately 6 inches long and 3/8-inch-thick were driven through His wrists; severing the sensorimotor nerves in each arm, producing unbearable bolts of pain. Jesus was then lifted up and the cross arm attached to the upright post. With His legs bent at the knee, a single nail was then driven through the arch of both feet. This too caused searing agony as spikes tore through nerves between the metatarsal bones and feet. Can you imagine this? Can you visualize His pain; imagine His bloody back, on the rough, wooden cross and the waves of unrelenting, throbbing pain coursing through His body as He hung suspended by spikes through His wrists? While He struggled, the onlookers and fellow victims hurled insults at Him. This is crucifixion. This is the cross. This price was paid for you and me.

What was the cause of Jesus's death? I remember the first time I heard that question asked in the small group I attended while in college. My guess was that Jesus bled to death or that He died from pain. The truth is that most people who were crucified suffocated. Hanging by their arms in this way created cramping and paralysis in the muscles that made it possible to inhale but not exhale. The sufferer would periodically push himself upward in order to change positions so that he could exhale and then settle back down into his previous position, and the process would start again. The waves of throbbing and searing pain, the panicky feeling caused by not being able to breath, the desperate attempt to push himself upward to exhale and take a short breath, this torment would repeat itself for periods of hours and sometimes days until the exhausted prisoner would succumb to the pain and die of asphyxiation. In Jesus's case, we know that it took roughly six hours for Him to die, eventually suffering from a ruptured heart. We know this because when His side was pierced after His death, both blood and water poured out, a sign of heart failure. All of this is what Jesus endured physically for you and me.

Matthew 26:52-53

52 "Put your sword back in its place," Jesus said to him, "for all who draw the sword will die by the sword. 53 Do you think I cannot call on my Father, and he will at once put at my disposal more than twelve legions of angels?

While being arrested, Jesus ordered His disciples not to resist, stating that if He desired He could summon twelve legions of angels to defend them. Now, I don't know how big a legion of angels is, but I do know that a Roman legion could be up to 6,000 men. I also know that it only took two angels to destroy Sodom and Gomorrah and a legion of angels is significantly greater than two. Twelve legions of angels are a lot of firepower. The fact is, Jesus could have prevented all of this, and once it started, He could have ended it at any time. When He was insulted, when He was slapped, when He was beaten, all He had to do was snap His fingers and all of it would have stopped. So, why didn't He? One reason, for persevering through His ordeal was to obey His father. But what else motivated Him? The answer to this question is found in the third way that Jesus suffered.

Jesus Suffered Spiritually

Matthew 27:45-46

45 From noon until three in the afternoon darkness came over all the land. 46 About three in the afternoon Jesus cried out in a loud voice, "Eli, Eli, lema sabachthani?"(Which means, "My God, my God, why have you forsaken me?").

Right before Jesus passed, He cried out in a loud voice, "My God, my God, why have you forsaken me?" Why would He ask that question? In the throes of His agony, had Jesus lost faith? No, Jesus, cried out because He was experiencing a different kind of distress. God really did leave Him, and for the first and last time in history, the two became separate. Why would God separate Himself from Jesus?

Isaiah 59:1-2

Surely the arm of the Lord is not too short to save,
nor his ear too dull to hear.
2 But your iniquities have separated
you from your God;
your sins have hidden his face from you,
so that he will not hear.

II Corinthians 5:20-21

21 God made him who had no sin to be sin for us, so that in him we might become the righteousness of God.

God is perfect. God is light. In Him is no darkness, no blemish, no sin. No one who has sinned can be in His presence, and no one whose hands are stained with sin will experience eternal life. The consequence of sin is estrangement from God and the penalty of sin is death.

God is loving, God is merciful, God is compassionate, but God is also just. For the fallen to be reconciled to Him, God could not just ignore sin, and nothing a fallen soul can do could make up for His offenses or heal the brokenness, which is their fruit. Justice demanded that someone had to pay the price. Someone who was perfect and without blemish had to die for all of us who had fallen. On the cross, Jesus took on all of our sin, becoming sin, becoming an atoning sacrifice for those who place their faith in Him. When this happened, when Jesus took on our sin, God separated from Him, literally and temporarily cutting off part of Himself. Jesus cried out the words in Matthew 27:46 as a result of that agony. With all the emotional and physical torment He suffered, I believe this was the greatest pain He felt, the greatest pain that anyone has felt since the creation of the world.

So why didn't Jesus stop the beatings, come off the cross, or send His angels just to wipe everyone out? Jesus had to die this way and at this time for any of us to have a chance to be saved. He stayed on the cross for us, for the hope that one day we would turn to Him and He could reconcile us to God and heal us. What I missed for so many years was the simple fact that Jesus did this for me and because of me. Yes, He died for the whole world, but if I'd been the only person who ever lived, He would have had to die to save me. My lies, my hatred, my immorality, were the nails in His hands and the whip on His back. I am Christ's murderer, and yet, as He gazed down from the cross at me, His betrayer, He loved me so much that He refused to come down. He wanted so badly for me to have a chance to be with Him forever that He endured the shame, the humiliation, and the beatings, all of it for me. Until, I made this personal, I could not understand it, and once I did, nothing was ever the same.

God/Jesus can tell me that He loves me but mere words can never express the width, length, height, and depth of His love. The cross is His love letter to me. It shows that He loved me first and loved me best, with a love that is unshakeable, unbreakable, and unimaginable. When I struggle with my self worth, I simply look at the price tag and remember the price that was paid for me, and the fact that I am truly and deeply loved, flawed and broken as I am. I can tell someone a myriad of different aspects of what is involved in having a relationship with Jesus, but there is only one why – the cross. The love letter took hold of me and refuses to let me go.

Before reading further, it is important to understand that everything that is written next hinges on whether someone believes in Jesus and believes in the reliability of the Bible's testimony about Him. If Jesus is just a man who lived two thousand years ago, then His death on the cross, while tragic, falls in line with many other human tragedies that populate human history. If Jesus is who He says He is and He did what the Bible says He did for you and me, well, that changes everything. I remember, shortly after I started attending that small Bible study group, taking time to ask myself what I really believed. I knew what I was taught. But did I have faith of my own? This was my red pill - blue pill moment (this is a *Matrix* reference for those of you not versed in Nerd). If I did not truly believe, I could take the blue pill and my life could go on as it always had. But if I believed, really believed that Jesus is God and He died for me, well that was something different. The message of the cross and what He did for me constituted the proverbial red pill. Jesus's love letter was the red pill that demanded that I make a choice, and once I accepted it, the cross propelled me on a faith journey that changed everything. I decided that I believed, and once I did, some stark truths became evident, and the love letter was at the center of it all.

Jesus has sent you a love letter as well, written with His blood at great cost. This kind of passion demands a response. So, what is the acceptable response to that kind of love? I'm glad you asked. That's a good question but one we are going to answer in the next chapter.

Chapter 4

Crazy in Love

I love you: three simple words but man, are they powerful. Once they are spoken, you can't take them back, and when they're uttered, everything about a relationship changes. That's a lot of pressure, and it's a scary thing to be the one to share those words first. What if he/she doesn't feel the same way? What if you ruin a perfectly good friendship by jumping the gun? Worst of all, what if you get the most dreaded response in the universe, "I like you too,"? Nothing can be worse than that.

Before getting married, I'd been involved in other relationships, and when they ended, I'd been the one to break it off...all except one. I'll never forget how things ended with my high school sweetheart. When we graduated, we went away to separate colleges. I had it in my mind that I was in love, and that we would continue our relationship long distance, graduate, and eventually get married. If I remember correctly, I'm pretty sure I had dropped those three magic words, "I love you," before we went away to school. Now, I went to college before the Internet, cell phones, and texting, so long-distance communication took the real commitment of writing letters and paying for long distance phone calls. Early in my first semester, I received a letter from my girlfriend. It was the dreaded Dear John, or in my case, the Dear Frank letter. The gist: Dear Frank, let's just be friends and see other people. What? Needless, to say I was devastated and no, if we weren't going to be together I did not want to be friends. In fact, I don't think we ever talked or saw each other again after that (never said I wasn't petty). In truth, there's a part of me that would rather have had her say *I hate you*, than to say *I like you,* and I don't think I'm alone in that. When you are in love, the other person being in *like* is not a consolation prize. In fact, it might be the cruelest cut of all. What does this have to do with our relationship with God? Everything.

God loved us first. He loves us best. Jesus wrote a love letter with His own blood communicating the extent of that love and making it possible to have a relationship with God through Him. He said it first, in big, bold capital letters, "I love you." So now, the ball is in our court. A relationship with Jesus is available if we want it and are willing to respond to His love letter. So, what is the appropriate response to someone who loves you so much that He is willing to die for you?

What does it take to please God? Financial giving? Regular church attendance? According to some, just acknowledging Jesus is enough. For others, if one simply believes in Jesus and has good intentions that will suffice. There are many different traditions and points of view, but fortunately, Jesus tells us clearly what He wants in His own words. The challenge for some is that His words are contrary to popular opinion and mainstream, contemporary religious thought.

Luke 10:25-28

25 *On one occasion an expert in the law stood up to test Jesus. "Teacher," he asked, "what must I do to inherit eternal life?"*

26 *"What is written in the Law?" he replied. "How do you read it?"*

27 *He answered, "'Love the Lord your God with all your heart and with all your soul and with all your strength and with all your mind'; and, 'Love your neighbor as yourself.'"*

28 *"You have answered correctly," Jesus replied. "Do this and you will live."*

Matthew 22:36-40

36 *"Teacher, which is the greatest commandment in the Law?"*

37 Jesus replied: "'Love the Lord your God with all your heart and with all your soul and with all your mind.' 38 This is the first and greatest commandment. 39 And the second is like it: 'Love your neighbor as yourself.' 40 All the Law and the Prophets hang on these two commandments."

What does Jesus want from us? Love. He wants us to love Him in return. In Matthew 22:40, Jesus says that all of the rest of the commandments are summed up by simply obeying the command to Love God and to adhere to the second greatest command which is to share God's love with others. When someone does this, he has taken the first huge step toward entering into a relationship with Jesus. Simple, right? One would think, but one thing that life teaches us is that love can be described as many things. Simple is not one of them. Anyone who has been involved in a serious relationship knows that being in love brings some serious challenges, some of the greatest stem from the fact that we all bring different definitions of love and different love languages.

I'm a cave man. I don't normally need verbal affirmation, gifts, and Hallmark cards to feel loved. My wife told me she loved me once, and I figure that if she changes her mind, she'll let me know. For me, being respected, being in a transparent relationship, being needed, being supported, being trusted are the things that communicate care. That's what love is to me, but I can't love my wife in the identical way. If I did, she wouldn't feel loved at all. In addition to the things I value, she thrives on constant communication, verbal affirmations, being cherished, and being made to feel special. For a relationship to work, one has to learn how his partner defines love and love him/her according to their needs. That leads us back to the greatest commandment. Left up to our best thinking, we would all come up with our own standard of what it means to truly love Jesus, but being in a relationship only works if our definition matches that of the other party. So, it does not matter how I define loving Jesus; it matters how He defines it. Fortunately, the scriptures offer a solution for this. In God's wisdom, the greatest commandment does not simply say to love God. It is much more specific than that.

Love =Lordship

The greatest commandment isn't to love God. It is to love God with all your heart, all your mind, all your soul, and all your strength. Jesus wants all of me. He does not want to be part of my life, like He is one of the four food groups from the old food pyramid. He wants to be my life. Loving Him with all of my mind signifies that my thoughts and my decisions all bow to him. Although figurative use of the heart has evolved over the last two thousand years, loving Jesus with my full heart surely includes loving him with all of my emotion and passion. So, what is involved with devoting all of my soul and strength to Him? Visualizing loving Him with my strength is fairly straightforward. It is a love that is going to require energy and action, not just fuzzy feeling and good intentions. Soul is a little harder to quantify, but however one wants to define loving with the soul, it certainly means that at my core I'm all His. So, once I adore Him with all of my heart, mind, soul, and strength, what is left? Nothing. Jesus doesn't want much, just all that we have. That is how He defines love. Simple, right?

Not only does Jesus want it all, in fact, He demands it. It is not just a command. It is the greatest command; all the others hinge on it, and there is no relationship with God without it. When Jesus taught this, it wasn't a new teaching. Not only was Jesus quoting Old Testament verses, Deuteronomy 6:4-5, if one looks carefully, the greatest commandment is a teaching that screams out of every page of scripture, from Genesis to Revelation. Unfortunately, it is buried and made mute by the empty monument called mainstream religion. If this command is looked at through the lens of religion, it is unreasonable and must be severely watered down to be consumed. But once I put my religion aside for a minute and gazed at these words through the eyes of a relationship, it made perfect sense.

What is the only acceptable response when someone says to you, "I love you with every part of my being, I commit my life to you, and I'd die for you?" As stated earlier, I'm pretty sure. "I like you a lot," isn't going to cut it. Not one of us would accept that as the answer, nor would we accept, "Well, I love you but not quite like that...I mean that die for you part is a little extreme." Beautiful vows pledging full, wholehearted devotion were read at our wedding, and I'm sure that if instead of saying, "I do," I had said, "I agree to most of it, most of the time," Michelle and I would not have gotten married. I may have left the church building with a black eye and some lost teeth, but I assure you, I would have left single. When we pledge full devotion to someone, we, rightly, expect the same in return, and if one respects himself, getting anything less is a deal breaker. If that is what humans expect from each other, why should the great God in heaven, creator of all the universe, tolerate less? He shouldn't and He doesn't.

Why was my Christianity broken? Jesus wrote me a love letter with His own blood, proclaiming His love for me and my response was, "I like you too." Jesus wanted me to be in love, and I was constantly putting Him in the friend zone, giving him my leftover time, leftover devotion, leftover obedience. Once I did everything that I wanted to do, I tried to fit Him in. Jesus wanted us to be one and I was not even a good friend. Truth is, I treated Jesus more like a *side chick*, someone to turn to when I needed something, when it was convenient, when I could sneak away from the real object of my devotion...me. That lifestyle made me a good, religious young man, fitting in with all of my church-going friends, but it was never going to lead to a relationship with God. Jesus's love letter demands a response, and the only acceptable response to that kind of love is to surrender everything. Surrender is the only thing that would ever get me through the front door.

At the heart of the greatest commandment is the fact that loving God means surrendering oneself to Jesus. There is a name for that kind of love: Lordship. Lordship is Jesus's love language. When we bow down before Him, and make Him Lord of every area of our lives, that is how we say to Him, "I love you, too." Lordship is the response the love letter demands; it is the kind of love that Jesus craves and deserves. So, what does this all-in love/lordship look like practically?

Luke 9:23-26

23 Then he said to them all: "Whoever wants to be my disciple must deny themselves and take up their cross daily and follow me. 24 For whoever wants to save their life will lose it, but whoever loses their life for me will save it. 25 What good is it for someone to gain the whole world, and yet lose or forfeit their very self? 26 Whoever is ashamed of me and my words, the Son of Man will be ashamed of them when he comes in his glory and in the glory of the Father and of the holy angels.

Luke 14:33

33 In the same way, those of you who do not give up everything you have cannot be my disciples.

In my opinion, Luke 9:23-26 is simply the greatest commandment broken down for dummies, and I don't know about you, but I'm thankful for that. When it comes to spiritual matters, I can be extremely dense and slow to comprehend. The problem isn't my mind (at least, not that I know of). The problem is that I have a stubborn, prideful heart that is quick to make excuses, exalt my own opinions and tradition, debate the obvious, and look for loopholes. If there is a way to misapply or water down a spiritual concept to make it fall in line with my preferences, my sinful heart will search for it. God, in His infinite wisdom, has written passages like Luke 9:23-26 for people like me, to cut through my spiritual clutter. It is so specific and so practical that even a spiritual dummy, like me, can't help, but understand it. Luke 9:23-26 breaks down the concept of all-in love and shows us, functionally, how it works. This passage is shocking in its bluntness, starting with the beginning of verse 23. In verse 23 Jesus says, *"whoever wants to be his disciple must...*" making it clear the directives that follow outline what is required for anyone who claims to follow Him, not just the *super Christians*. Verses 23-26 aren't just a good idea, they define what it means to be a Christian.

Verse 23 goes on to state that we must deny ourselves take up our cross daily and follow Him. What comes to mind when you think of denying yourself, and I don't mean just in a spiritual context? Have you ever denied yourself for something? The answer is yes, right? We all deny ourselves for things that we love or deem important. Parents deny themselves sleep in order to meet the needs of their children; students make sacrifices in order to graduate college; people go to work, even when they hate it, in order to get a paycheck. The list goes on and on. Anything that I've loved or prioritized has required sacrifice. Well, here's the thing, for so long, God had seen me pull all-nighters for parties, for school, for my friends, etc., seen me drive for hours in order to impress some girl, and seen me do just about anything to make a buck. Yet, when it came to serving God, unless serving him was convenient, I didn't do it. Would I go to church? Sure, if church wasn't too far, I wasn't too tired, or there was nothing more urgent happening. Would I read the Bible? Of course, if I wasn't too busy with work or school, nothing too good was on TV, the stars were aligned just right, and I absolutely had nothing on my social calendar. Would I follow God's commandments concerning my personal morality? Definitely, if they weren't too unrealistic, if people didn't push me too far, if her dress weren't, oh, so tight, I'd definitely obey. Jesus isn't stupid. He saw how I treated the things that were important to me, and He saw how I treated Him. When I came to understand Luke 9:23, I saw that Jesus drew a very simple line in the sand. Loving Jesus meant making Him Lord, and making Him Lord meant that I needed to deny myself for Him. Trying to pass on my half-hearted love as love was going to be a deal breaker. If I wanted a true relationship with Jesus, I needed to put what

He wanted ahead of what I desired. In any relationship, denying self is what you do for the one you love, and if the call is to love Jesus with all of my heart, mind, soul, and strength, than surely it meant that His demands needed to supersede anything else in my life. In a successful relationship one does not do things that he knows will hurt his partner and he makes every effort to do the things that please his better half. So it is with Jesus. Denying myself for Him meant saying no to sinful practices, behavior that I knew caused Jesus to die for me on the cross, and it meant making time for the things I knew brought Him joy. Real love is an action word, a radical word that forces revolutionary change. A real relationship with Jesus requires real love. Lordship=love.

This concept is further elaborated upon in the rest of verse 23. Jesus tells us that in order to be His follower we must take up our cross daily and follow Him. Like most people, my first thought when I read this part of the passage was that carrying my cross daily meant fulfilling my Christian *burden*, going to church, being a nice guy, etc. To understand what Jesus is really saying, one has to read His words from the perspective of His immediate audience. For me, and most of us today, the cross is an object on T-Shirts bumper stickers, church buildings, and historically inaccurate paintings, where Jesus is carrying it on His back, with great difficulty. For the audience of Christ's time, the cross was simply a brutal instrument of death. The only time someone would ever carry the patibulum of his cross is when that person was going to be nailed to it. When Jesus spoke these words, it was clear to His listeners that carrying your cross daily meant to die daily. That takes the concept of denying myself to a whole new level.

What does it mean to die to myself, daily? It means that if I choose to follow Jesus, my life is no longer my own. Every day, I nail my sins, my plans, my opinions, even my dreams to the cross and put Jesus's before my own. The next day, I get up and do it again. Why daily? Because my sinful nature and my willfulness are like Jason from the Friday the 13th films. Every time I kill it, it comes back to life and starts chasing me around my house. If I am going to live for Jesus and not for me, this is a decision that I need to reaffirm daily. That daily decision to die to me and live for Him is part of what it means to carry the cross daily, but this is not the entirety of the matter.

The other aspect of His statement is less figurative and more literal. For the first three centuries of Christianity, it was often an outlaw religion, and Christians lived in constant fear of persecution. The ill-treatment for Christ's followers could come in *mild forms* such as being the objects of ridicule, being banished by their families, and cast out of the synagogue. Then there was the harsher treatment of being arrested, beaten, losing their jobs, or having their property confiscated. The very worst forms were being stoned to death, being turned into human torches, being fed to lions or wild dogs, or being crucified. These Christians had to be prepared, literally, to carry their cross daily, never knowing if and when they would be asked to make the choice to renounce Jesus or die. Many chose to die rather than to renounce Jesus even one time, reasoning that it was better to be with the one they loved than to betray Him. Wow, amazing faith, right? So, what does that have to do with us? That type of thing doesn't happen today, does it? Well, yes it does. Unfortunately, there are still places in the world where being a disciple of Jesus means embracing life-threatening risks, and for these Christians, this passage is still very literal. But even for the overwhelming majority of Jesus's followers, who will never be in such extreme situations, it is still very relevant to our faith and to the understanding of Luke 9:23.

Imagine me on judgment day in line, waiting for judgment. In front is a Christian who was crucified for his faith two thousand years ago and behind me is one who was martyred last year in an Iraqi jail, sandwiched in the middle is me. Those two were willing to die for Jesus. How can I claim to have made Jesus lord if I do not have same heart that they had? I will hopefully never have the same circumstances, but shouldn't I have the same heart? Isn't the acceptable response to someone who died for you to be willing to die for them as well? I'd die for my wife. I'd die for my children. If Jesus is truly lord, shouldn't I have the heart to die for Him?

Why is this important? Because at the point that I am willing to die for something, I am fully devoted, and I am really ready to live for it. Carrying my cross daily means that I make the daily decision to be all in. If I love Jesus with full devotion, I will go anywhere, change anything, do anything for Him because once someone is willing to die, there are no limits to what he will do for the one he loves. This is what Luke 9:23 is communicating. This is crazy talk if you look at devotion through the prism of religion, but isn't this what it means to really be in love?

When I lived in Atlanta, I had a neighbor who had a teenage son who lived in California. One day his son called him and said he was in love with some young lady he had just met. His dad told his son that he definitely was not in love. His son protested. They went back and forth for a little. Finally, his dad asked his son if he was willing to die for the young woman. His son said, "No." His dad replied, "Then you don't love her. Love means that you are willing to die." That is certainly how I feel about my family. Because I am willing to die for each of them, I am willing to serve them, change for them, and even go on midnight runs to buy personal lady items for them (Is there anything more embarrassing for a guy? You know that's love). On the day I give each of my two daughters away in marriage, I cannot imagine giving either away to a man who does not love them as passionately. Why do we expect Jesus to want a lesser kind of love?

So, is Jesus asking for perfection? Of course not. I can't be perfect but I can be fully devoted. Since the first day that I professed my love to my future wife, Michelle, I have been

100% devoted. It took Michelle about five minutes to figure out that I was not perfect, but flawed as I was and am, I was all hers. God is making us the greatest deal in creation. I bring my broken-down life to Him, surrender that life fully, and He will wipe away my sins and give me a new life here and eternal life to come. Imagine if you had an old car, say like a 1997 Honda Accord. Imagine if someone was willing to trade you a 2018 62-S Mercedes-Maybach Sedan for your Honda, no strings attached, no money owed. There is only one catch. You must trade in your car and all the stuff in it, if you hold on to anything, the deal is off. So, you can have one of the top luxury cars in the world for free in exchange for your broken down vehicle and the junk inside of it. Would you do it? Can you imagine calling off the deal because you wanted to hold on to your air freshener or your spare tire? That would be crazy, right? Well, God is willing to give each of us an even better deal, but we have to give Him full control of our lives to get it. This is God's grace in action. Some may ask, "How can this be grace if we have to give something to God to receive it?" Simply put, grace is a free gift, not a free ride.

Grace is one of the most discussed and least understood concepts in the Bible. We all know that we need it, but sometimes it seems that no one can decide on exactly what it is and how it works. In one sermon, a preacher will read from Ephesians 2:8-10 and proclaim that we are saved by grace not by works, only to turn to II Corinthians 5:10, a few minutes later, and instruct his congregation that each one of us will be judged according to his deeds. Huh? So, which is true and if both statements are true, how exactly does that work? Understanding lordship and the greatest commandment is at the heart of grasping the practical application of grace and how it relates to salvation.

Merriam Webster defines grace as help or kindness that God gives or shows people. BibleTools.com states, "An accurate, common definition describes grace as the unmerited favor of God toward man." My personal definition expands on the concept of unmerited favor. In my opinion, grace stems from the simple truth that God is love. Grace then is the essence of God's divine nature, the practical manifestation of His love. In regard to humans, every manifestation of His love is unmerited because we are never worthy. In many cases, His favor toward us is unconditional but not always. Daily, God demonstrates the aspects of His grace that are unconditional to both sinner and saint alike. Examples of unconditional favor would be being born, being alive, being of good health, etc. The grace of salvation however would be an example of conditional favor.

Salvation, i.e. being rescued from the penalty of sin, is reserved for those who have responded to the message of the cross and who, through Jesus, have been brought into a covenant relationship with God. Through God's grace and Christ's sacrifice, the opportunity to be saved exists for everyone, but this divine gift, while unearned, has conditions. If this were not the case, everyone would automatically be saved, regardless of his or her beliefs or actions, and just a cursory reading of scriptures will prove that this is not the case. What people often confuse is the concept of something being conditional and something being earned. When someone works a job, his or her wages are earned. They are being compensated, hopefully fairly, for the work they have done. Grace is not a wage. Grace is an undeserved gift but even something undeserved can have provisions. If I were to find a winning lottery ticket for one hundred million dollars on the street, would that be a wage? Is there anything that I've done to deserve it? Depending on your belief system, it is simply sheer luck or pure divine blessing. Still, if I wanted to actually receive my winnings, there are things that I have to do (like sign the back of the ticket, drive to the lottery office, show my I.D., etc.). Failure to follow these instructions would mean a failure to receive my blessing. The fact that I have to follow these directives would not diminish from the fact that my lottery winnings were a free gift. Salvation works exactly this way. The truth is that the New Covenant, like the Old has terms, different terms, and simpler terms, but terms nonetheless. So, what are the conditions that God places on entering into a covenant relationship with Him? Well, the greatest commandment is at the heart of it. Lordship is the first huge step towards accepting God's grace.

God perfects us, through Christ's blood, in response to our full devotion. I surrender my broken life to Him and receive eternity and healing. God's grace in action is His unmerited love toward me, that He is willing to grant me unparalleled riches and immeasurable love in exchange for the toxic dust that is my life. There is only one string attached. He wants all of me.

Once I understood this, the scriptures confronted me with two questions. Had I ever made Jesus lord of my life? No, for me the answer was clearly, no. OK, that being the case, was I willing to make Him lord? Big decision, biggest decision of my life. I needed to count the cost (Luke 14:28-33 talks about this) and weigh it. Everything about me would change if I did this. If I gave up control of my life, I knew it would involve changes. Even without knowing the particulars, that was a scary proposition, and I knew that it would involve surrendering my path and my carefully crafted future plans to Him. I had the perfect plan: Graduate with honors, attend Harvard law school, become a hotshot lawyer, make tons of money, marry Jane Kennedy (if you don't know why that was a big deal, you're just too young), go into politics, and change the world. Making changes was scary but surrendering my future to Jesus was out right terrifying. So, what were the pros? On the cross, He'd already proven His love. Did I trust Him? Was there anything in my life worth holding on to that would justify missing the deal of my life? Did I honestly believe that I could write a better script for my future than Jesus? Making the choice to make Jesus lord and love Him according to His love language was the best decision I have ever made. Because no matter how much I give, I can't out give Him, and I can't out love Him. Besides, He's better at running my life than I am.

Chapter 5

Being Exclusive

It is a scary thing to give your heart fully to someone and take a chance and say, "I love you," not knowing how that person will respond, but you know what's even scarier? Someone, saying, "I love you, too." It is exhilarating and wonderful and extremely terrifying, a true relationship game changer. With it comes a new set of expectations, some spoken, and some unspoken. For most couples, this involves some type of exclusive relationship, each one with its own unique tone and idiosyncrasies. Like in a romantic partnership, making a decision to love Jesus plunges us into an exclusive relationship, one with its own set of rules and expectations. To help us explore those expectations, it's best that we define some terminology.

What is a Disciple?

Acts 11:25-26

25 Then Barnabas went to Tarsus to look for Saul, 26 and when he found him, he brought him to Antioch. So, for a whole year Barnabas and Saul met with the church and taught great numbers of people. The disciples were called Christians first at Antioch.

If you did a survey in your community and asked people what it means to be a Christian, what kind of answers might you receive? What responses might you get if you asked what it means to be a disciple? Are they the same thing or something different? One of the great dilemmas facing modern Christianity is that everyone seems to have his own personal definition for being a Christian. Further confusing the matter, though the term disciple is gaining in popularity in many circles, for most it still is a term cloaked in mystery. Acts 11:25-26 offers some clarity. The events in Acts 11 take place approximately thirteen years after the establishment of Christ's church in Acts 2. For thirteen years, Christ's followers had been moving around, spreading the gospel. Well, Acts 11:26 tells us that the first place people were ever called Christians was in Antioch. Since this is the case, what were they called for the first thirteen years? Again, the answer is found in Acts 11:26. The passage states that the disciples were called Christians first at Antioch, meaning that prior to being called Christians, Christ's people were simply known as His disciples. Originally, Christian was just another name given to people living the life style of a disciple. Why is this so important? It is extremely valuable because it allows us to have a Biblical standard for defining and evaluating our Christian walk as opposed to relying on the shifting sands of opinion or the conflicting traditions found in organized religion.

When searching for a Biblical definition of a Christian, little can be learned by doing a word study on the term Christian itself since it only appears in the Bible three times, Acts 11:26, Acts 26:28 and I Peter 4:16. Fortunately, the term disciple occurs in the New Testament alone well over two hundred times. Since the term Christian was assigned to individuals devoted to living as Christ's disciples, a study of discipleship gives great insight into true Christianity. Simply put, a true Christian is first and foremost a disciple of Jesus.

As stated earlier, with a romantic couple, falling crazy in love leads to a radical change in the relationship. In most cases, a decision is made to have some kind of exclusive, monogamous relationship, and each couple needs to establish its own rules for what is and isn't acceptable. This is true for being in love with Jesus as well. Once we make Jesus Lord and respond to Christ's love by fully devoting ourselves to Him, Jesus calls us into an exclusive relationship with Him. This relationship is called discipleship. With this being the case, it is imperative to understand what Jesus expects from His disciples. Perhaps the best place to gain some insight is studying Jesus's interaction with some of His first disciples.

Lordship Leads to Discipleship

Mark 1:16-20

16 As Jesus walked beside the Sea of Galilee, he saw Simon and his brother Andrew casting a net into the lake, for they were fishermen. 17 "Come, follow me," Jesus said, "and I will send you out to fish for people." 18 At once they left their nets and followed him.

19 When he had gone a little farther, he saw James son of Zebedee and his brother John in a boat, preparing their nets. 20 Without delay he called them, and they left their father Zebedee in the boat with the hired men and followed him.

In Mark 1:16-20, Jesus calls Peter, Andrew, James, and John to be His disciples. This passage, and life in general, breaks down to *the what* and *the why*. The *what* examines the particulars of what Jesus is calling His disciples to do, and the *why* explores their motivation. All in love/lordship is the why, that crazy love is what inspires and drives discipleship. So, what exactly does the call to discipleship entail?

The first and foremost aspect of the call is found in verse seventeen as Jesus declares, "Come follow me." Disciples are individuals who have decided to follow Jesus anywhere He leads them, for the rest of their days. This means following Jesus in reality, not just with our good intentions. Before grasping this and becoming a disciple, I was a classic example of someone who followed Jesus in theory but not in reality. I did not know the Jesus of the Bible well enough to follow in His steps, and I had a half-hearted commitment to obeying what I did know. This is not the call that Peter, Andrew, James, and John answered. They were tasked with literally following in Jesus's steps.

Those men walked where Jesus walked, served when Jesus served, preached where Jesus preached, healed where Jesus healed, and were persecuted when Jesus was persecuted. Clearly, the call to follow Jesus is a call to imitate Him, like the original disciples, imperfectly but with full devotion. For a disciple, the question, "What would Jesus do?" is not merely a slogan; it is a blueprint for life. Discipleship is a daily decision to strive wholeheartedly to treat my family as Jesus would, to make decisions with His moral integrity, to be a reflection of His generosity, His compassion, His grace, and His purpose. At my best, devoting myself fully to living out His blueprint, I still fall far short, but when I fall, I accept His grace, learn from my failings, get up, and start again. Before I understood discipleship, I would use my human frailty as an excuse for lukewarm commitment and indifference to Biblical commands that I deemed too difficult. I reasoned, since I couldn't be perfect, as long as my intentions were good, I was OK. I would say to myself, "At least I was trying. I'm one of the good guys. Most people don't even do that." I call this religious logic.

Can you imagine if I applied that same logic to my marriage? Hey, since I can't be perfect as a husband, if I have an affair, she'll understand. I still love her in my heart. No, that kind of religious logic does not work in marriage. That kind of thinking would get me divorced, shot, or worse. In my marriage, being imperfect is not an excuse for a lack of devotion. As much as I may blow it, I make every effort to please my wife and would die before I would betray her. No, that doesn't make me perfect, far from it (the road to our nearly twenty-nine years of marriage is paved with my apologies), but it does make me a devoted husband. Relationships require devotion and true devotion is displayed through giving wholehearted effort. We all know that there is a huge difference between trying and making every effort. If someone invited me to a party, I might try to make it. If it's not too late, not too far, I'm not too tired, nothing else interesting is happening, I might come. If my house catches on fire, I'm not going to *try* to get out. I am going to make every effort, exhaust every possibility. My religious logic reasoned that as long as I made some token attempt to be spiritual, it would be enough, as if I was doing God some enormous, cosmic favor even to give Him any attention. Discipleship calls me into an exclusive relationship where my unrivaled love for Jesus is displayed in my unwavering devotion toward walking in His steps. Sometimes I walk, sometimes I run, sometimes I am too weak and my Lord carries me on His back until I can get up and hobble along. But every day I give all my heart, all my mind, all my soul, and all my strength to follow my Lord, to go where He leads me, to imitate Him, no turning back.

Disciples Have a Purpose

The decision to follow brings us back to verse 17 where we learn another important dynamic of discipleship. Jesus says, "Come follow me and I will send you out to fish for people." Following Jesus did not only give His disciples a new direction; it gave them a new purpose. Whether their former lives had been purposeless or full of purpose, Jesus was calling them to a new life mission. Their prime directive now that they had decided to become disciples was to help others become disciples also. This should not be surprising. How could someone endeavor to walk in His steps and not adopt His passion for the lost?

Luke 19:9-10

9 Jesus said to him, "Today salvation has come to this house, because this man, too, is a son of Abraham. 10 For the Son of Man came to seek and to save the lost."

Jesus's stated purpose was to find and save the lost. Everything He did was intentional, driven by His mission to make a way for us to go to heaven and help as many as possible get there. Pat Riley, back when he was the coach for the New York Knicks, famously said, "The main thing has got to be the main thing." What was Jesus's main thing? Saving the lost. Yes, Jesus, fed the hungry, and healed the lame, but Jesus's main thing was getting people to heaven. So how can I be a disciple of Jesus if that is not my mission as well?

Now, this is not the version of *Christianity* I was raised in. In my view, it was OK to believe in Jesus and to discuss Him among likeminded people but going around trying to recruit people was intrusive and weird. People who went around the neighborhood or campus initiating unsolicited conversations about Jesus or aggressively inviting people to their church or small groups were Jesus Freaks and had taken Christianity much too far. I talked in the first chapter about how God used a small group at the University of Maryland to save my soul, and how it was instrumental in teaching me about discipleship and having a real relationship with Jesus. Well, I didn't find that Bible study group on my own, and honestly, I wasn't looking for one.

There were an overwhelming number of religious groups on campus, and I made it my point to avoid all of them. I considered myself a Christian, but I was taking a break from organized religion and reasoned that there were better uses of my time. I bumped into a student named Steve Johnson who, enthusiastically, invited me to a Bible study held in Elkton Hall on Mondays in one of the dorm rooms. He was passionate, so I told him I would attend in order to get out of the conversation, knowing that I would never come. I remember thinking, "Nice guy, maybe too nice, you'll never catch me being some Jesus Freak, recruiting strangers or hanging with people who do." In my mind, that was the end of that. There were 37,000 undergraduate students at Maryland. What were the odds of bumping into him again? Well, God has a sense of humor, and He was pursuing me. Steve and I had no classes in common and lived on separate areas of campus, but somehow, it seemed like I would bump into Steve once or twice a week, and every time he'd be just as nice and invite me to the same small group, Mondays 8PM at Elkton Hall. Every time, I'd pretend as if I'd forgotten and lie about coming to the next one, with no intention of ever showing up. It was like *Groundhog Day* (great movie if you haven't seen it). I don't remember how many times this went on before he wore me down, and I finally showed up for no other reason than to stop him from inviting me. I thank God for Steve and his perseverance. Most of what is good in my life had its origin in that small group on that Monday night. Steve was a disciple of Jesus, and I am thankful that he answered the call. Fishing for men and women and bringing them to Jesus does not make someone a Jesus Freak. It makes that person an ambassador for Christ and a hero, who rescues the lost and the strays and brings them to Jesus. What is challenging is that Jesus's proclamation in Mark 1:17 makes it clear that for true Christianity/discipleship, this is not the exception. It is the standard.

Jesus called Peter and others to follow Him and said that He'd make them fishers of men. Can you imagine if Peter had replied, "I'll follow you but that fishing for men stuff is not for me. I'm not good with people. That's not my personality." Do you think that would have been acceptable? Of course not. The Christian walk involves embracing Christ's mission. That does not mean that every disciple needs to quit his job and become an itinerant preacher, but it does mean that disciples need to see the world around them and their place in it differently. There is a reason that once someone is saved he is not taken immediately to heaven. God leaves us here for a purpose. Every disciple is in the heaven business; the goal being to run the race, make it to heaven, and help as many people get there as possible. If this is the case, where I live, where I work or go to school is not simply random. It is the mission field that God has chosen for me. Every disciple is a missionary, an ambassador for Christ, proclaiming the gospel with his life and his words. Who falls in love and does not profess it to the world? Crazy love inspires disciples to follow in Christ's steps and proclaim His love to a broken world. These are two of the defining characteristics of discipleship. These principles are evident in Mark 1:16-20, some of the first words Jesus spoke to His disciples, and they are evident in His last words as well.

Matthew 28:18-20

18 Then Jesus came to them and said, "All authority in heaven and on earth has been given to me. 19 Therefore go and make disciples of all nations, baptizing them in the name of the Father and of the Son and of the Holy Spirit, 20 and teaching them to obey everything I have commanded you. And surely, I am with you always, to the very end of the age."

Sometime after Christ's resurrection and before His ascendance, Jesus gave the above instruction to His disciples, commanding them to go make disciples of all nations. This passage is called *The Great Commission.* It contains the marching orders for God's people, both collectively and individually. Dissecting these verses will give us further insight into the life of a disciple. What is clear from verse nineteen is that to go make disciples is a command not a request.

Clearly, Jesus demands all of us who follow Him to share our faith as we go, to be intentional about it and to teach others *the what* and *the why* of becoming His disciples. Disciples are followers who make disciples, spreading the love of Jesus like a virus comprised of saving grace. The reality of sharing Jesus is not just a disciple sharing the gospel but his life as well; this process is personal and it is intimate and it is soul-to-soul, heart-to-heart. No church program or campaign can be a substitute for the individual passion of each Christian to make disciples, and truthfully, those of us who profess to be a Christian but do not embrace the call to make disciples, are simply following a different Jesus than the Jesus of the Bible.

I shared in the first chapter that modern Christianity is broken, and the neglect of the Great Commission lies at the heart of what is defective. Too many churches focus on membership and not discipleship. I heard a preacher say recently, "God did not call us to make members. He called us to make disciples," and he could not have spoken a timelier truth. Discipleship transforms lives, but a person can be a member of a church for decades and lack real joy, saving faith, or deep conviction. A pastor can build a megachurch of 30,000 members and have only a nominal effect on the community, but two-thousand years ago a handful of disciples changed history. Swelling memberships can build beautiful, sprawling buildings, but disciples making disciples has and will turn the world upside down. Why? Relationship is more powerful than religion, lordship is more motivating than tradition, purpose is more potent than programs, and love is far more essential and enduring than routine. The call to make disciples is the balm for much of what ails the modern church and a bridge that can transport the willing from religion to relationship.

The next part of the command is to make disciples of all nations. This speaks to the scope and the heart of the command. The goal is to present everyone on earth the opportunity to make Jesus Lord and to teach the willing how. However, to accomplish this, disciples must learn to love how Jesus loves. Our eyes must become colorblind, culture blind, class blind, and politics blind, seeing the world through the prism of Christ's blood rather than through our own ingrained cultural biases, prejudices, and agendas. Dr. Martin Luther King Jr. once said, "It is appalling that the most segregated hour of Christian America is eleven o'clock on Sunday morning." Fifty years later, this statement is still, heartbreakingly true. If we can answer the call of the great commission to share Christ's love to all, we will see these walls come tumbling down.

Looking at the next section of the command, it tells us to go make disciples of all nations and baptize them. In this verse, Jesus makes it clear that baptism is involved with the Great Commission, and that it is part of the process of making disciples. The religious world is unnecessarily divided on the topic of baptism, and Jesus's words here should provide some much-needed clarity. After someone makes the decision to be Jesus's disciple, He is commanded to be baptized. This teaches us two important insights about baptism. The first is that baptism is important to Jesus, and secondly, that a candidate for baptism is someone who has first made a decision to be Jesus's disciple. More information about baptism and its role in discipleship is revealed in other passages, but here we receive these two important building blocks to serve as a foundation to our understanding of the subject.

The remainder of the command instructs that the newly baptized disciple is to be taught to obey everything. This is another important aspect of the Great Commission. New converts should not be abandoned like orphaned children, forced to fend for themselves as they navigate a new life. Jesus makes it clear that the role of a disciple is not just to find and teach individuals so that they can become Christians but to mentor young disciples after conversion and help them develop toward spiritual maturity. This investment of love and concern will bear abundant fruit as the young disciple matures into a disciple who makes disciples. It is truly a gift that keeps on giving. A church full of disciples is a relational network that is a family brought together by grace and purpose. This does not describe the church of my youth, but it does describe the Christianity of the Bible.

This all can be overwhelming, and even what I've shared is by no means an exhaustive list of what is involved in being Christ's disciple. So, before you drop this book and run out of the room, take a deep breath. The key is to focus on *the why* and not *the what*. For the married people reading, you can understand this. If someone had given me an accurate list of everything that was involved in marriage when I was single, I'd probably still be single. If someone had given me an exhaustive list of every detail involved in parenting, I would have never had kids. The truth is, seeing my bride-to-be open up those church doors and start down the aisle (an image that still gives me chills), the details of what was expected from me were the last thing on my mind. All I could think of was that I loved her, and I'd do anything for her. It was the same when each our two daughters, Jacquelyn and Kenya, were born. Holding them, my heart was filled with so much love. How could I hold my daughters and not be all in? Once I fell in love, real love, everything else was just details. At that point, I was fully invested. Focus on the love, and the rest comes easy.

This is the same for our walk with God. If you haven't done it yet, take the time to get to know Jesus and fall in love with Him. If you focus on *the what* and lose sight of *the why*, you will end up with empty, burdensome religion, and that never saved anyone. Decide on *the why* and *the what* comes easy. Yes, disciples are called to imitate Christ's life, and yes, we are called to make disciples, but that is not really the point. The point comes down to three simple questions. Does Jesus love you? Do you trust Him? Do you love Him enough to give your life to Him? If you want my advice, do not focus on the details of what God expects until you decide what your answer is to those three questions. The why has to come first. If you get to know Jesus, the real Jesus, gazing into the heart of the one who died for you, you will fall in love. How can you help but be all in? How can you help but to surrender all to Him and share this love with others? This is the essence of the two greatest commandments; everything else hangs on these. Focus on the love and the rest comes easy, everything else is just details. With that being said, I am not trying to minimize the fact that Jesus cares very much about us being obedient to these details. But truthfully, once someone is motivated by Christ's love, obedience to His commands is a joy not a burden.

The remainder of this book is dedicated to practically examining Jesus's expectations for His disciples, and how our Lord gives so much more than He demands. Signing up to follow in Jesus's steps is a journey that will lead to a life of transformation and healing on earth and eternal life to come.

Additional Scriptures Concerning Discipleship

Luke 9:23-26, Matthew 22:37-40, Luke 10:25-28,

Luke 14:25-33, Luke 9:57- 62, Luke 13:22-25,
Mark 1:16-20, John 8:31-32, Acts 11:25-26,
Matthew 28:18-20, John 13:34-35

Chapter 6

The Engagement

Being engaged is the time in a relationship where everything becomes more serious - DEFCON 1 Level serious. The idea of sharing vows and making a permanent commitment to someone is equal parts exciting and daunting. For one thing, wedding planning is a dizzying, mind-boggling adventure. No matter how much time a couple has to plan for it, it is never enough; there are so many details. There are even more specifics to discuss when two people are working through the particulars of merging their lives. Topics that may not have been breached or even thought about, now, have to be carefully vetted. My place or yours or do we get a new place together? What furniture are we keeping? How do we manage our finances? Everything, I mean, everything is about to change. To the unmarried men contemplating matrimony, let me give some life advice. It is far more valuable to make your bride happy than to have your way. Don't be too attached to your favorite couch, that comfy chair, or even that favorite sweater (my wife took me shopping and gave me a makeover when we got married; I never saw it coming). It is different for every couple, but the one constant is simply this: for two people to come together, some stuff has to go, and some new things are going to be added.

So, how does this relate to having a relationship with God? Well, because I love Michelle, I am willing to make changes in order to please her and to cut off behavior that hurts her. Becoming a disciple is the greatest decision anyone can make and it is the most important. As with marriage, this decision is motivated by love, but also, like marriage, when someone decides to follow Jesus, he has to make a decision to subtract some behavior from his life and add some as well. These choices are motivated by a desire to please God and to avoid behavior that saddens Him. Still, regardless of motivation, change is hard. Before making this commitment, one has to decide whether the benefits of following Jesus are worth enduring the challenges. The Bible refers to this process as counting the cost.

Luke 14:28-30

28 "Suppose one of you wants to build a tower. Won't you first sit down and estimate the cost to see if you have enough money to complete it? 29 For if you lay the foundation and are not able to finish it, everyone who sees it will ridicule you, 30 saying, 'This person began to build and wasn't able to finish.'

The scriptures make it clear that failure to count the cost will often result in failure to complete our Christian walk. We all understand that the biggest decisions of our lives cannot be just emotional choices. So, if choosing to follow Jesus is life's most significant commitment, doesn't it stand to reason that before deciding an individual should make an informed decision and weigh the pros and cons? So, what are some of the important issues to consider when deciding to become a disciple?

The arguments for discipleship bring me back to *the why*. Christ's love for me and my love for Him are at the top of my list, but love is not the only impetus, nor was it the first one that resonated with me. The fear of hell was my first motivator, and the promise of heaven was the second. And, still, thirty-four years later, my belief in the reality of heaven and hell are important catalysts that help keep me centered, especially during those times when I have struggled and felt disconnected from Christ's love. As I moved forward in my faith, I have discovered many other inspirations that keep me excited about my choice but those three are what inspired me in the beginning. Surprisingly, when it comes to additional reasons to be a disciple, some of the most inspiring are found among the aspects that gave me apprehension.

What made me nervous about discipleship boiled down to two things: the thought that the moral changes being demanded were too extreme and the fear of failure. They loomed over my head consciously and subconsciously as pretty intimidating costs of following Jesus. Funny thing though, the more I read the Bible and the more I let it reveal my need, these *costs* became some of the most compelling reasons for becoming a disciple.

Marriage is like this too. A healthy marriage has a multitude of sacrifices that are really unexpected blessings. I mentioned previously how the day after I was married, Michelle started revamping my wardrobe. If someone had told me that this was going to happen six months earlier, I would have been offended and defensive. I considered myself a decent dresser (I was a lousy dresser), with great taste, (I had none). I would have asked, "Why should I sacrifice my distinct style, my individuality to please my wife?" It would have seemed like I was compromising what made me, me. Why would I have responded that way? Because I was under a powerful delusion. Sense of style? I dressed as if I was homeless, and everyone knew it but me. After we got married, Michelle flashed her mesmerizing smile and batted her big brown eyes, and the next thing I knew my clothes were in the dumpster. Before I could work up a good case of indignation, I turned and looked in the mirror and realized that she was much better at dressing me than I was. So, you tell me, what exactly did I sacrifice?

Following Jesus is exactly the same. The Biblical name for my feared, big *cost* is repentance. Jesus calls those who would be His disciples to repent, to make a decision to turn from the sin and vices of their old life and embrace a life of following Him. For me, the idea of putting my old life in the dumpster was a deal breaker, but it only seemed that way until I saw my life through sober eyes. Like many, my pre-disciple perspective of my life was one big, powerful delusion. Under this delusion, I thought my life was fine even if it wasn't, claimed to be happy even when I was hurting, and rationalized that I had things figured out even when I was totally clueless. No matter how much I was drowning, I really wouldn't allow myself to see it. I was a spiritual hobo, who felt he had a sense of style.

Earlier, I said that the Bible study group helped change my life during my sophomore year. This is true, but I attended for the first time during the fall of my freshman year. Steve invited me out over and over again. I eventually came and was very skeptical, but I ended up loving the group. It was very practical, something different about the people, in a good way. I Was excited to come back the following week, somewhat to learn more but mostly because there were some pretty girls attending, (don't judge me). After a few weeks, Steve asked me if I wanted to get together and look at a few scriptures some time. I said yes, and later on that week we did. It did not go well. I wish I could say it was him. I wish I could say that Steve was rude, or weird, or obnoxious, or Jim Jones crazy, but I can't. The truth is, he showed me some scriptures that I hadn't seen before, and they convicted me. I was convicted by the content and ashamed of the fact that I knew so little about the Bible. Did I admit that? Of course not. I got mad and debated him, trying to prove that I knew as much as he did (I knew nothing but you know how we Davises love to debate). After a while, I stormed away, mumbling to myself that I wasn't going to let some self-righteous Jesus dude judge me. The fact that Steve had been nothing but kind and far from judgmental wasn't the point. Never confuse a good argument with the facts. He being so nice made it worse. I knew what he was thinking, blasted Jesus Freak. I vowed I'd never go back to the Bible study group. Why was I so mad? The scriptures that he shared with me showed me something about myself, poking a hole in my delusional bubble, and it was easier for me to make Steve the enemy than to look at me. My bubble and I were just fine the way we were. It was a whole year before I attended the small group again. Why did I come back? The scriptures I had heard and the joy I had seen during my time attending the group and in my conversation with Steve followed me and started eroding my bubble.

I was sobering up. Have you ever attended a party where there was heavy drinking? Than like me, you know from experience that things get pretty wild. Now, have you ever attended a wild party and been completely sober the whole time, not one touch of alcohol or any other drug? I have. It is a surreal experience. I wasn't a drinker, so my friends used to have me bartend some of the parties, to serve the beer and keep them from doing anything, life altering, stupid. Seeing people blasted, slobbering drunk, making fools of themselves, when you're abstaining, takes people watching to new heights. It is a good thing that smart phones, Facebook, and You Tube had not been invented back then. What's really funny, is that people who have had a few drinks and think they're sober or just a little *buzzed,* end up being some of the worst offenders. They act completely out of character and are just as susceptible to really stupid decisions as the rest of the crowd. See, you can't see yourself clearly, when you're under the influence. It takes sober eyes to see.

Twelve months can be a long time and a lot of things happened. I did some things, things I thought I'd never do, of which I am not proud and hurt people close to me. Prior to that year, no matter how bad my life was, I couldn't see it, at least not until I was exposed to those scriptures, and once I was exposed, I couldn't shake them. They sobered me up just enough that I started to feel my own misery. I felt my emptiness, my loneliness, my anger, and my guilt. For the first time, I would look in the mirror and see glimpses of my true reflection, and I hated the man I had become. I sat in it for twelve months. I hadn't been to the group in a year, hadn't bumped into any of the members on campus (I told you, God has a sense of humor). One day I just decided I needed help. I remembered that they had the group on Monday nights and prayed that it was still there. Through God's grace, it was still at the same place and time (I found out later that the Bible study often changed locations each semester and had just moved back there). I attended that week and the next, like a man walking out of a desert finding a stream. I don't know if Craig, one of the guys who attended, approached me or I approached him about getting together during the week, but I was eager. I knew I needed help, and if facing ugly truths was the price of being delivered from them, I was all in. See, I realized two undeniable truths during those twelve months I was away. Truth one: I was broken. Truth two: I did not have a clue how or the means to fix myself. Changing in my broken life for a new one no longer struck me as a cost; it was an act of grace. It was time to put the old Frank in the dumpster and become something new.

So how does that work, exactly? The culprit, that was slowly, insidiously, destroying my life was this little thing called sin. What is sin? AllAboutGod.com answers the question, thusly, "The truth is that sin, as defined in the original translations of the Bible, means 'to miss the mark.' The mark, in this case, is the standard of perfection established by God and evidenced by Jesus. Viewed in that light, it is clear that we are all sinners." For my money, this is an accurate and fairly succinct definition. If one understands sin Biblically, sin is not just the *big ticket* items, murder, rape, adultery, etc. and it is so much more than a case of crime and punishment, with God waiting to pass judgment on us unless Jesus can somehow get us off for good behavior. Shockingly, the Bible reserves the same punishment for the murderer, the coward and the liar; the same judgment for acts of commission, acts of omission, and vile thoughts, and the same grace for all the above if the offender is willing to repent. This raises some serious questions.

I remember wrestling with all manner of questions about God's commands and from my worldly perspective so many of the rules themselves seemed extreme and unfair. What type of God would send someone to hell for rape and someone else to the same place for consensual sex outside of marriage or let the murderer who repents into heaven and keep a watcher of porn who doesn't out? That didn't seem fair. God could not actually expect anyone to break his back trying follow all the commands in the Bible, could He? I mean, really, lust is a sin? How is that even possible? Lust was my favorite past time, hardwired into my DNA. He made me this way so how was He going to judge me for doing what came naturally? What was next, breathing? Who did He actually expect to be able to follow all of this? And if the answer is no one, what is the point? Who writes a test that no one can pass?

I learned the definition of sin as a child in Sunday school. The truth is, understanding the definition of the term did not give me understanding. It simply left me vacillating among confusion, guilt, and apathy. My view of God vacillated too. Sometimes He was an unreasonable, legalistic, judge, sometimes He was a cool Rasta granddad with dreads that let things slide, and other times He was an absentee father, letting the world and more importantly, my world, fall apart. And how did grace fit into all this, anyway? If I am saved by grace, can I just charge it all to my grace credit card and keep on living my life? Does my grace card have a limit? In lieu of clarity, like most people, I simply made up my own rules. According to my rules, different sins had different weight. If I just avoided doing the really bad stuff, did very little of the medium stuff, and kept the rest discreet, God and I would be OK. That sounded fair. The problem was that my way didn't work, and as a result, my life was crashing down. So, what is the truth about sin and repentance?

We Are All Broken

Romans 3:23

23 for all have sinned and fall short of the glory of God,

Isaiah 59:1-2

Surely the arm of the Lord is not too short to save,
nor his ear too dull to hear.
² But your iniquities have separated
you from your God;
your sins have hidden his face from you,
so that he will not hear.

My views of God, grace, sin, and repentance were a big part of the problem. I had to get beyond my Sunday School teachings and the theology of the *Church of Frank* and learn what a relationship with God truly entailed. I learned that God is not the rule police, who wrote the Bible to take away my fun and weigh me down with a plethora of demanding and impractical commands. In fact, I needed to start looking at the Bible less like a book of laws and more like an operator's manual for my life.

If I buy a car, I have a choice. I don't have to read the instruction manual, and if I read it, I do not have to do what it says, but if I ignore it, it will lead to my vehicle breaking down. Some actions, like driving without brake pads, will break my car quickly. Other actions, like ignoring my oil light and not checking my oil, will damage it more gradually, but at the end of the day, any form of neglect will lead to the same result, me taking Uber, with my car in the shop.

Sin leads to brokenness. Whether it is *big sin* or the yellow flashing light that we call *little sin*, it breaks and erodes every part of us and everything that we touch, causing the earth itself to groan and beg for Christ's return. Like with any operator's manual, we are given the freedom to ignore the Bible's instructions, but our spiritual neglect has consequences for us and everyone around us. According to Isaiah 59:2, sin divides. It severs our relationship with God, demolishes our friendships, implodes our marriages, poisons our children, and breaks us to the very core. What starts as fun, escape, convenience, or curiosity, ends in tears and desperation, leaving us shaking our heads and wondering, "How did I get here?" As Romans 3:23 states, we have all sinned. We are all broken, broken toys who take turns at the bottom of life's toy box, pointing fingers at each other as we pass judgment on whose sin is worse. Sin is both our pusher and our drug. The pusher spends years helping us sample from his inventory until we find our drug of choice. Then, we become addicted to the drug, losing ourselves in its *tender* embrace, as it *lovingly* sucks the light out of us, stealing our clarity, our character, and our conscience. It steals it all until each of us is a hollow shell of the young boy or girl who was going to change the world. Now, we are the world.

It is not a question of what sin is worse. What many of us consider a small sin is often just an entry point, the spiritual equivalent of a gateway drug, destined to lead our hearts further into the dark woods. Most spouses do not set out to be unfaithful. *Harmless* flirting leads to *innocent* daydreams, which leads to lunchtime conversations about each other's spouses, which leads to an emotional affair, which leads to…Everything starts somewhere. Besides, talking about a small sin reminds me of that old joke about minor surgery. What is the definition of minor surgery? The answer: surgery that is done on someone else. If the doctor is cutting into me, it is always major. Sin is exactly like that. The sin that has its hooks in me, that won't let me go, that is always the most serious. It is unconstructive to compare my journey to anyone else's. The goal is to understand and conquer the vices that are derailing me and keeping me from being the person that God created me to be.

Sin is the gift that keeps on giving, a curse that can condemn generations of families to live out the same destructive cycles or in other cases, mutate to form new patterns, inspired by the first. Alcoholics can give birth to meth heads that give birth to prescription drug abusers. The verbally and physically abusive spawn progeny who express their emotions through razor sharp tongues or fist or not at all, locking them away until they fester like a cancer of the soul. The idolatrous father, who worships his career, sacrificing his family on its altar, will find himself married to a stranger and the patriarch of emotional orphans. Generational curses are real and can be difficult to break. Hurt people hurt other people, and broken souls perpetuate brokenness. I should know. I am a child of a generational curse.

When I was eight, my parents divorced and for all intents and purposes, I ceased to have a father that day. Initially, he moved to Baltimore, about forty minutes away from us, but even after we moved to Baltimore as well, we had very limited interaction. Sometime before my tenth birthday, he remarried and moved to California, and from that time until I graduated college, I probably saw him less than four times and spoke to him by phone less than a handful of times a year. My mom did a great job as a single mom, raising four children, three boys and a girl, all three years apart, but we still had some rough times and an intense transition.

I had two childhoods. When my parents were married, we lived in ritzy suburbs, always one of the few African-American families in whatever neighborhood we were in. My dad was a doctor and my mom was an educator, and every day after school I'd go outside and play with the Jodies, Buffys, and Kips who populated the neighborhoods of 1970's suburban Maryland. One school year after the divorce, my mom realized that she could not afford the suburbs and moved us to Baltimore, 1970's Baltimore. I was definitely not in Kansas anymore. Now, my friends were Tyrone, Nene, and Peaches, and I quickly needed a new set of survival skills. Fun times. In the midst of this, we had a household full of love, but also full of more than its share of drama.

We never missed a meal, but we did have some creative ones. Candle light dinners (not the romantic type, the no power type), government cheese sandwiches, tons of hand-me-downs, and five years with no heat in the house, are just some of our adventures. One Christmas, during the years we had no heat, we woke up to find large ice sickles hanging from the bathroom ceiling. It was a negative three degrees outside. Meanwhile, my dad lived in Diamond Bar, California in a house in a gated community that had a pool, a tennis court, and between twelve and fifteen TV's (I counted them the one time I visited but I don't remember the exact number). I don't share these details to vilify my dad or to paint my childhood as some tragedy (It wasn't, far from it). I simply share this to paint a picture of my state of mind and how the dichotomy of our lives and our father's life tormented me. For example: I remember that during the winters of my last three years of high school that I would sleep in my thick winter coat, a knit hat, and mittens, on the bottom bunk of the bunk bed that I shared with one of my brothers. On more than a few nights I would lie down and watch my breath in our icy room and think about our father, and I can assure you my thoughts were not happy thoughts. The dark side of the force was calling out to me and I was listening.

I was consumed with anger. It was fueled by pain, pain caused by feelings of abandonment and rejection, a deep feeling of inadequacy, fear, and most of all by love. My dad had been my idol and he was gone. Why would he do this? Why cut us off? What was wrong with him that he would walk away from his children? What was wrong with me that he did not want me? I hated him; I loved him; I wanted desperately to hurt him; I wanted him to hug me; I pretended he was dead; I craved for his approval, swimming in a whirlpool of emotions that I could not process and would not acknowledge. And all that unprocessed hurt manifested itself in two things that I could understand: fear and rage. They were with me every morning and slept next to me every night. They fueled my accomplishments and poisoned my relationships. I tried to hide my two companions from prying eyes, putting on the façade of the nice guy, the happy, well-adjusted, achiever, but my twin demons were always there, barely hidden under the surface. Unfortunately, demons can only stay hidden for so long, and by my college years, mine were starting to bear fruit.

When my parents were together, people would always tell me that I reminded them of my father, and I remember how proud it would make me feel, how I'd walk around wearing his giant hat from his time in the army, pretending to be him. After the divorce, being like dad became an insult. I tried desperately to run the other way, but by making life choices driven by bitterness and insecurity, I wasn't running away from the curse. I was running toward it.

So, was my dad a monster? No, he was just a man, a man suffering from a very specific brand of brokenness. I don't want to speak for him, but I do not think that it is a coincidence that my dad was raised without his physical father, abandoned by him. It is not hard to imagine my father lying on his bed, feeling many of the things that I had felt, learning all of the wrong lessons from his father's failings. I am not excusing my dad's shortcomings any more than I can excuse my own. I am just highlighting a spiritual truth. Sin kills; sin destroys; sin breaks, and the repercussions of our sinful choices poisons us, our children, and our children's children. As a result, we often, unknowingly, become the thing we hate, learning the wrong lessons from our pain, because we see the world through a broken lens.

That was my story. As a college sophomore, I was hurting and I was making decisions that were hurting others. My fear made me a relational chameleon, becoming someone different in every setting, constantly terrified that anyone would look beyond my façade. My anger and insecurity gave birth to a myopic ambition and a silent but deadly Machiavellian streak, that was more than willing to betray friends to serve my greater good.

There is a famous parable about a frog. The parable states that if someone puts a frog in boiling water, it will jump out but if the temperature is turned up gradually, the frog will stay put and be slowly boiled to death. Sometimes, that is how sin operates. Slowly, insidiously, it gradually changes us into someone unrecognizable. In my case, I was turning into the kind of man who was attempting to medicate his pain through achievement and willing to hurt others in the pursuit. Who did that sound like? I couldn't see it. I was in denial about my pain and I was always able to rationalize my every action, remaining the hero in my own story. In all likelihood, my delusional downward spiral would have continued, but God in His grace had better plans for me. He made sure that I crossed paths with disciples who could show me a better way. They showed me how to break the curse.

Brokenness Can Be Good

Romans 7:24-25

24 What a wretched man I am! Who will rescue me from this body that is subject to death? 25 Thanks be to God, who delivers me through Jesus Christ our Lord! So then, I myself in my mind am a slave to God's law but in my sinful nature a slave to the law of sin.

Jesus is the curse breaker. Jesus, through the shedding of His blood, rescues us from the penalty of our sins, and through the gift of the Holy Spirit, empowers us to overcome both our sin addictions and the damage that our choices and the choices of others have caused. There is no person, no self-help book, and no success strategy, that can heal the wounds and repair the walls that have been torn down in us like Jesus can, and there is no penance we can perform to earn our forgiveness. However, as we established in chapter four, the fact that we are saved by grace does not mean that salvation is unconditional. The gifts of forgiveness and empowerment are available to the whole world, but each individual must take hold of this grace to benefit from it. As shared in the same chapter, lordship, surrendering oneself completely to Jesus, is the key to our response. When we surrender our sin and our brokenness to Jesus, it takes on a different name: repentance. The scriptures make it clear that repentance is both a necessary step in the salvation process and an integral part of the lifestyle of a disciple once he is saved. So, what is repentance, and how does someone go about repenting of his sin?

Luke 13:2-5

2 Jesus answered, "Do you think that these Galileans were worse sinners than all the other Galileans because they suffered this way? 3 I tell you, no! But unless you repent, you too will all perish. 4 Or those eighteen who died when the tower in Siloam fell on them—do you think they were more guilty than all the others living in Jerusalem? 5 I tell you, no! But unless you repent, you too will all perish."

The scripture above and many others, clearly, articulate the importance of repentance. It is both the key to healing and refreshing and a necessary step in accepting Christ's grace. In an article for ThoughtCo.com, Jack Zavada offers the following definition, stating, "Repentance in Christianity means a sincere turning away, in both the mind and heart, from self to God. It involves a change of mind that leads to action--the turning away from a sinful course to God."

The Eerdmans Bible Dictionary defines repentance in its fullest sense as 'a complete change of orientation involving a judgment upon the past and a deliberate redirection for the future.

Ultimately, although most people normally discuss repentance strictly in terms of turning from sin, it really encompasses every aspect of the decision to leave one's old life and fully dedicate himself to being Christ's disciple. In many ways, repentance is a synonym for lordship or surrender, but it has inherent in its definition the practical application of those concepts. If Jesus is truly lord, then radical changes need to take place in order to conform to His example. These changes involve every aspect of our lives, both thought and action. Lordship demands that some habits must be cast off and others must be added, and repentance is the decision to follow through on the promise of Jesus being lord by surrendering the details of who we are to Him.

Luke 13:2-5 makes it clear that there is no salvation without repentance, no being born again until we decide to kill and bury our old lives. I've heard it said that salvation is achieved by simply accepting Jesus as your personal savior, but Jesus did not request permission to be my savior. He demands to be my lord. When Jesus became my lord, He became my savior because everyone under the authority of His kingdom is redeemed by Him. For so many years, I wanted the benefits of God's eternal kingdom without fully submitting to His authority. In his masterful book about repentance, *Repentance: A Cosmic Shift of Mind and Heart*, Edward Anton reminds the reader that both John the Baptist and Jesus open the proclamation of the gospel with the command, "Repent for the kingdom of heaven has come near." Of this, Anton writes, "For only a cosmic shift of worldview affords us a view of the kingdom of heaven." Without repentance, a relationship with God is impossible.

One of the most comprehensive passages concerning the subject is II Corinthians 7:8-11.

II Corinthians 7:8-11

8 Even if I caused you sorrow by my letter, I do not regret it. Though I did regret it—I see that my letter hurt you, but only for a little while— 9 yet now I am happy, not because you were made sorry, but because your sorrow led you to repentance. For you became sorrowful as God intended and so were not harmed in any way by us. 10 Godly sorrow brings repentance that leads to salvation and leaves no regret, but worldly sorrow brings death. 11 See what this godly sorrow has produced in you: what earnestness, what eagerness to clear yourselves, what indignation, what alarm, what longing, what concern, what readiness to see justice done. At every point you have proved yourselves to be innocent in this matter.

The above passage outlines the process and motivation of repentance. Many individuals confuse repentance and contrition, but repentance is much more than feeling guilty about ones sins or the state of one's life. That being said, contrition does have its place and II Corinthians 7:8-11 explains its role.

Unless someone's heart is completely calcified, coming face to face with the pain and damage caused by his transgressions and the effects of sin on his life will bring about regret and sorrow. Sometimes the regret is over the consequences of his failings, sometimes it is induced by taking responsibility for the hurt he has caused God and others, and sometimes it is a little bit of both, but anguish and heartbreak are common to anyone who has been honest with himself, looked beyond the veil of denial, and glimpsed his own wretchedness. Sorrow is common to man. The question is whether the sorrow is worldly or godly.

Verse 10 makes it clear that worldly sorrow leads to death. Why? In many cases, it does not lead to turning to God as the solution, and in others, it only inspires lip service to a godly life. Worldly sorrow can produce guilt, depression, bitterness, obsession, or superficial, religious piety, but it will never inspire true devotion to Jesus. Even when worldly sorrow is directed toward Christ, its effects are only temporary, often creating an endless loop of indulgence and regret. There is an old quote/poem often shared by critics of Christianity that describes this cycle.

"A Christian is a man who feels
Repentance on a Sunday
For what he has done on Saturday,
And is going to do on Monday."

What the author of this quote mistakenly labels repentance is truly worldly sorrow and a pretty accurate description of it as well, and what he mistakenly labels Christianity is merely empty religion. Worldly sorrow and false Christianity are conjoined twins, that promise everything and produce nothing of consequence. Life is not found in dead religion; it is found in Christ alone, and worldly sorrow will never lead someone to Him. Godly sorrow, however, is something entirely different.

When someone allows God's truth to shine a light on the darkness inside him and does not turn away from or make excuses for what it reveals, not only will he see clearly the brokenness of his life, he will be broken in spirit as well.

Psalm 51:16-17

You do not delight in sacrifice, or I would bring it;
you do not take pleasure in burnt offerings.
17 My sacrifice, O God, is a broken spirit;
a broken and contrite heart
you, God, will not despise.

As this passage illustrates, brokenness can be a good thing. When an individual honestly evaluates his life by the standard of the scriptures and takes full responsibility, it can lead to the type of godly sorrow expressed in this passage and in II Corinthians 7:8-11. This contrition will lead him to turn away from his old life and surrender his life to Jesus.

II Corinthians 7:11

11 See what this godly sorrow has produced in you: what earnestness, what eagerness to clear yourselves, what indignation, what alarm, what longing, what concern, what readiness to see justice done. At every point you have proved yourselves to be innocent in this matter.

Godly sorrow produces repentance and repentance inspires radical action. The individual who repents does everything within his power to change. The addict flushes the drugs down the toilet, the philanderer cuts off relationships and deletes contacts off his phone, the liar comes clean with the truth, and the bitter, young college sophomore decides to forgive. Imperfect people are incapable of repenting perfectly, but as with every aspect of lordship, Christ's disciples fully devote themselves to the process, making every effort to turn from self and embrace discipleship. Repentance is both the decision that a disciple makes at the beginning of his race and a daily choice. The Bible functions as a disciple's spiritual GPS, and as one's life veers off course, repentance will allow him to course correct. The promise of this radical mind change is to become a new creation, but while the individual supplies the desire and willingness to change, the power comes from somewhere else.

Acts 3:19

19 Repent, then, and turn to God, so that your sins may be wiped out, that times of refreshing may come from the Lord,

Repentance is our part, but the heavy lifting belongs to Jesus. As Acts 3:19 clearly states, the wiping away of our sin and the times of refreshing come from the Lord. Try as we might, even making every effort, we cannot change ourselves, the roots go too deep, and the call of our inner demons is too strong. We cannot break the chains of sin, heal the wounds from our past, or learn a new way of being simply on willpower and determination. It is the redeeming power of Jesus's blood that washes away our sins and the supernatural power of the Holy Spirit that makes transformation possible. But this is the interesting part; God respects our free will. He will not deliver us until we desire it with all of our heart and soul. Repentance is an acceptance of God's grace and an invitation for him to act on our behalf.

I imagine that God was working throughout my life, trying to get my attention, longing for the day when I would truly turn to Him. He longed to redeem my soul and heal my wounds and to free me from my anger and fear, but He needed me to do something first: surrender. Once I truly understood, surrendering to Him was not a cost. It was a rescue. But before I could get to that point, I needed to take a long hard look at the scriptures and see what they said about me. The Bible is a mirror and it will show us ourselves, our true selves if we let it. There is no transgression too egregious, no addiction too strong, no wound too severe, and no curse too dark for God to overcome. He is able and willing to save. The question for me and for all of us is are we ready to repent, or at the very least, are we ready to take a good look in the mirror?

At the end of this chapter, there are additional scriptures concerning sin and repentance. My encouragement is to look over the scriptures concerning sin and search for yourself. Find the passages that speak to your misdeeds, your brand of brokenness, your pain, and when you do, study them, apply them to your life, learn their lessons. Afterwards if you have a desire to move forward, I recommend three things. First, spend time praying about what you've found and ask God to give you godly sorrow and clarity. Second, begin to study the passages on repentance. Third, find a spiritual mentor, someone with spiritual maturity that you can trust and entrust him/her with assisting you in the process of learning how to embrace discipleship fully. For someone new to discipleship, this can be a life changing process, but even for seasoned disciples, these passages are a powerful reminder that can strengthen your walk. A new life is waiting. It is not a life without challenges, but the blessings far out weigh the challenges, and many of our tests are simply blessings in disguise.

Additional Scriptures Concerning Sin

Galatians 5:19-21, Mark 7:20-23, Romans 1:24-32

I Corinthians 6:5-11, I Corinthians 6:15-20, James 4:17

James 5:16, Luke 18:9-14, Ephesians 5:3-13

Matthew 5:27-30, Hebrews 10:26-27, Colossians 3:5-11

Ephesians 4:29-32, II Timothy 3:1-7, Revelation 21:8

Genesis 4:6-7, Romans 7:14-25, Matthew 18:21-35

Additional Scriptures Concerning Repentance

Luke 13:1-5, Luke 3:7-14, Acts 26:20

Isaiah 57:15, Colossians 3:12-14, Acts 3:19

II Corinthians 7:8-11, Psalm 51:16-17, Romans 8:5-13,

Acts 2:36-38, Psalm 51

Chapter 7
The Wedding

The wedding day: what a special day. Michelle and I had a fabulous wedding. OK, honestly, I don't remember most of it. It was a blur, and I was an emotional mess. The one thing that I do remember and I will never forget is when the doors of the church building opened and Michelle started walking down the aisle, with sunbeams and angels ushering her in. Wow, I almost had a Denzel Washington man tear go down my cheek. It was an amazing moment. In this world, there is no shortage of opinions about marriage and weddings, and among them are an increasing number of voices that argue that marriage is not essential, but the Bible leaves little room for ambiguity.

God created marriage and He likes weddings. In Ephesians 5:21-33, Matthew 19:1-12, and elsewhere, the scriptures share God's views on the subject. For Him, marriage is essential, a permanent, binding covenant between a man and a woman. Over the years, I've spoken with many couples where one party (generally the man) disagrees and would minimize the importance of matrimony. Many a man has told me some version of the following, "What's the big deal about getting married? I love her; she loves me. We live together and function as husband and wife in every way. What would be different if she had a ring? Why does God care if we have some stupid ceremony? Aren't we married in the eyes of God?" I reply by answering the last question first. No. You are not married in the eyes of God. After that, I show the couple scriptures and teach them about God's views on the subject, and I talk to the man privately about the real reasons he is avoiding marriage because there is always a deeper reason. One of the legitimate, under-lying questions people have on the subject is how can a ritual mean so much to God? By definition, isn't a ritual merely symbolic?

The wedding is a ritual, but not all ceremonies are created equal. My wedding band is purely symbolic; other than tradition and sentimental value, it has no meaning. Placing it on my finger was part of our ceremony, but taking it on or off does not affect whether I am married or single. The wedding itself, however, is something different. The Bible does not give a specific procedure for marriage. The actual make-up of the ceremony is different for every culture, and the Bible passes no judgment on this, but it does place enormous value on a couple following their cultural customs, obeying the laws of the land, and declaring their union before God and man. Yes, marriage is a ritual, but it is not merely symbolic. The scriptures say that the two become one flesh and cautions, "Therefore what God has joined together, let no one separate"(Matthew 19:5-6). The two start the ceremony single and leave married. There is no magic in the venue, the officiant, or the words spoken. The ritual has power because God makes it so. Through an act of grace, He bonds two souls and seals them in a covenant relationship during that moment and time. It is a gift and a promise that He reserves for those who stand before Him in holy matrimony. I guess He could do things differently. He could offer this gift to anyone who whispers, "I love you," under the sheets, lives together for a period of time, or has a joint checking account, but He has chosen not to. God is sovereign; two becoming one is His gift to give, and He has chosen to empower the ritual of marriage and reserve His blessings and this gift for those who partake in it. We can argue with Him, but in the end, the voice of the Alpha and Omega is the only one that matters. Now, I'm sure you're wondering what this detour about marriage has to do with building an intimate relationship with God. It has more to do with it than most people think. Jesus instituted His own version of a wedding between Him and His disciples, and many of the same principles apply.

The Wedding Matters

Acts 2:37-39

37 When the people heard this, they were cut to the heart and said to Peter and the other apostles, "Brothers, what shall we do?"

38 Peter replied, "Repent and be baptized, every one of you, in the name of Jesus Christ for the forgiveness of your sins. And you will receive the gift of the Holy Spirit. 39 The promise is for you and your children and for all who are far off—for all whom the Lord our God will call."

In Acts 2:37-39, during the first sermon on the first day of Christ's church, members of the crowd asked, "What shall we do?" The context of the passage makes it clear that they were asking what they could do to be right with God. Peter's reply, "Repent and be baptized for the forgiveness of your sins. And you will receive the gift of the Holy Spirit." We know that repentance is a necessary step toward accepting God's grace. But what is baptism and why was it included as part of this response?

What is baptism? The simple answer is that baptism is an immersion in water. In an article written on the topic, Dr. Douglas Jacoby states the following, "The Bible shows people going into rivers to be baptized; going down into the water; and participating in something that parallels burial (Mark 1:5; Acts 8:38; Rom 6:4). There wouldn't be any need to wade in the water to be sprinkled with a few drops. Despite the biblical evidence, a number of denominations still hold that sprinkling or pouring is just as valid as immersion. What light is shed on the matter by the ancient languages?" Jacoby continues, "Baptidzo= immerse. (Often spelled baptizo.) The word always used for N.T. baptism. (It comes from the verb bapto, which means to dip.) Baptidzo literally means dip or immerse (in the active voice) and dip oneself, plunge, sink, or even drown (in the middle voice). Classical Greek authors used this word to describe ships sinking in naval warfare. The clear implication is total immersion."

So, the command in Acts 2:38 is to repent and be immersed in water, and the stated promise is that forgiveness and the gift of the Holy Spirit will be given to those who obey this command. Acts 2:39 states that this promise would extend from that day forward and would apply for all who would seek to follow Christ. Consistent with these passages, every example of Christian conversion recorded in scripture from Acts 2 forward involves baptism, and the central message of Acts 2:38-39 is echoed in other verses on the subject.

John 3:3-6

3 Jesus replied, "Very truly I tell you, no one can see the kingdom of God unless they are born again."

4 "How can someone be born when they are old?" Nicodemus asked. "Surely they cannot enter a second time into their mother's womb to be born!"

5 Jesus answered, "Very truly I tell you, no one can enter the kingdom of God unless they are born of water and the Spirit. 6 Flesh gives birth to flesh, but the Spirit gives birth to spirit.

Someone becomes saved when he is born again. That is the moment that a lost soul crosses over from darkness to light, and no one will ever see the face of our Lord and enter the kingdom of God who has not been reborn. With this being the case, Nicodemus's question in John 3:4 becomes the most crucial question imaginable. How can someone be born again? Jesus answers that being born again means being born of water and spirit. There is water in the plan. If John 3:5 is examined in isolation, many different theories about what it means to be born of water can develop, but if, like me, one believes that the entire Bible, ultimately, has one author, the Holy Spirit, the passage is easily understood. Once, John 3:5 is read in the context of similar verses, particularly verses which answer the same question, the ambiguity vanishes and its meaning becomes clear.

Both John 3:3-5 and Acts 2:37-39 are written to answer the same question. How can someone become right with God?

John 3:5 tells us that being born again involves being born of water and spirit and Acts 2:38 promises the gift of the Holy Spirit and the forgiveness of sins for those who repent and are baptized. It seems logical that the water referenced in John 3:5 is the water of baptism, the spirit discussed in John 3:5 is the Holy Spirit, and that being born again happens when an individual receives the promised absolution of sins and the gift of the Holy Spirit. The fact that more than a few additional verses concerning baptism (Romans 6:4, Acts 22:16, Galatians 3:26-27, Colossians 2:11-12, I Peter 3:20-21, Mark 16:16, etc.) link it to the salvation process provides further evidence supporting this conclusion. When all of this is coupled with the role of baptism in the conversions recorded in the book of Acts and the urgency with which those baptisms took place, I believe that the scriptures leave little room to doubt that immersion in water is an integral part of God's plan.

At this point, I want to repeat my encouragement from chapter two. I strongly recommend that every reader put aside any preconceptions on this topic, take some time to study theses scriptures, and come to his own conclusions. Please, do not take my word on the subject or for that matter anyone else's, and don't read these scriptures with a predetermined conclusion in mind. Additional verses are listed at the end of the chapter. Please, take your time and study them. When I first studied these passages, I was in disbelief because what I was reading contradicted what I had always been taught. I remember staying up most of the night, reading every verse on baptism in the Bible, and looking at every Christian conversion (Every recorded Christian conversion is contained in the book of Acts), trying to look for a way to justify my previous beliefs, but the more I read the more I realized something. There was nothing confusing or controversial about these scriptures. Acts 2:38 is one of the most straightforward and easily understood commands in the Bible. The fact that it wasn't what mom and grandma had taught me did not change the words on the page. At the end of the day, I had to decide whether I was going to try to bend the scriptures and make them say something more familiar or bow down before God's commands and trust in His promises over religious tradition or my own wisdom. Like it or not, baptism is part of God's plan. Still, the knowledge left me more than a little unsettled. I found myself asking how all this works, and why would our lord put so much emphasis on someone being immersed in water? Romans 6:3-4 sheds some light on why baptism is important and teaches us some of the mechanics of how baptism works. As in all things, let us start with the why.

Romans 6:3-4

3 Or don't you know that all of us who were baptized into Christ Jesus were baptized into his death? 4 We were therefore buried with him through baptism into death in order that, just as Christ was raised from the dead through the glory of the Father, we too may live a new life.

We cannot give ourselves a new life, and redemption is not a product of our deeds or any good work. The only thing in the universe that could ever be powerful enough to redeem a broken life, cleansing it of all sin, is Christ's death, the shedding of His blood. When we are washed in His blood, all our sins are forgiven, and we begin a new life. This gift is available for everyone, but only those who accept the gospel can take hold of it. That brings us to an important question. According to scriptures, how exactly does someone become united with Christ's death and at what point and time does a believer get washed in the blood of the lamb and become born again? Romans 6: 3-4 teaches us that the point in time where this takes place is baptism. When we repent and turn to Him, we die to our old lives, when we are lowered into the waters of baptism, we are buried with Him, and as we are raised up out of the water, we are raised to live a new life. We become one with His death burial and resurrection in the waters of baptism. How can this be? Is baptism some great work that earns us redemption? Of course not. In fact, the person being baptized does very little other than humble himself to Christ's command and trust in His promises. Baptism is neither a spiritual work nor a mere symbol. It is a ceremony, but not all rituals are created equal. Baptism is a wedding, the most important wedding of our lives. It is the point and time where a disciple unites with Jesus's death and is born again in Him.

Like any wedding, there is no inherent power in the act itself. The power is not found in magic water, human action, the person being baptized, or the person performing the baptism. Human logic tells us it is an act that should have little significance. What difference could being immersed in water possibly make? If someone has made the decision to make Jesus Lord, why should Jesus care if this person is baptized or not? It is just a ritual, an outward sign of an inward grace, right? It is a ritual God created as the act that seals a covenant between Him and His disciple. The Lord has chosen to require a simple ceremony where someone professes Jesus as Lord before God and man. Through an act of grace, Christ empowers this ritual so that what happens in that moment is binding on heaven and earth. Under the water is the place where the disciple shares the tomb with Jesus, his covenant with his Lord is signed in blood, and the disciple's spiritual DNA is rewritten. Salvation is a gift and a promise that the Lord reserves for those who are surrendered and who submit to this simple command. He could choose to do things differently. Jesus could have instructed us to pray a special prayer or dip seven times in the river Jordan, but those are not the instructions He has given. God is sovereign, and He has chosen to empower this ritual and insure His blessings and this gift for those who repent and partake in it. We can argue with Him, but in the end, the voice of the Alpha and Omega is the only one that matters.

The truth is, nothing about this should be difficult or controversial. I truly believe that if one takes the time to study these scriptures, they are among the most straightforward in the entire Bible, and the act of baptism itself takes very little effort. But Satan conspires to distract people from righteousness, and when distraction is not possible, he works to confuse those who seek it. One of the schemes that Satan deploys with baptism and other Biblical teachings is the use of *what if* scenarios. Maybe, you are thinking through a few of your own.

What if someone loves the Lord sincerely and is never baptized? If I accept this view of baptism, what about all those who came before who believed differently? Are you saying that these righteous men and women weren't saved? Many of my spiritual heroes living now have not had this view. Does this teach that they are wrong? Does this teach that these men and women who love God dearly are somehow unsaved? These are legitimate questions, questions that I needed to reconcile in my own mind when I studied these verses. These are also emotional issues, and I know from experience that emotions can cloud my eyes to obvious scriptural truths and allow me to hear other voices other than the Holy Spirit. Having these questions is not what gets us in trouble. What often gets people in trouble is answering these questions based on our own understanding and building a theology around what makes sense to us. There are many reasons why there are thousands of separate denominations under the Christian banner and building theological houses based on hypothetical scenarios often plays a major role. We want answers, and if the answers the scriptures give us are unpleasing or incomplete, we often devise our own. With that being said, these legitimate questions deserve serious study and prayer. Let us examine some of these and the Bible's response to them.

Deuteronomy 29:29

²⁹ *The secret things belong to the Lord our God, but the things revealed belong to us and to our children forever, that we may follow all the words of this law.*

Deuteronomy 29:29 is one of the most challenging scriptures in the Bible and adherence to it is one of the keys to walking a godly path and avoiding the pitfalls of false theology. What this passage states is that the Bible is God's revealed will to man. It is everything that mankind needs to know to have a relationship with God, but what is revealed is only a fraction of the mind and will of God. God gives information on a need to know basis. He expects us to trust and obey completely the truths that He has passed on to us, and He also calls us to trust Him to handle the mysteries and numerous unanswered questions. If God did not deem to share the answers, the answers belong to Him, and He fully expects us to trust in His ability to handle these issues with grace and justice. Put differently, He wants us to handle our business and stay out of His. Why is this challenging? Because as humans, we feel like it is our right to know everything.

We want to know everything and often feel like it is our right, and in the absence of knowledge, we are hesitant to trust. It is this combination of arrogance and curiosity that Satan exploited in the garden when he manipulated Adam and Eve to question and disobey God's command concerning the Tree of Knowledge. God gave a simple command concerning the tree and not a lot of details. He did not satisfy Adam and Eve's curiosity and answer all of their *what ifs*, and Satan slid into that gray area and planted the seeds of distrust and disobedience, showing them a more *reasonable* way then what they had been told. Ever since the garden, this has remained one of Satan's favorite strategies. God expects us to trust Him. He calls us to search the scriptures for answers for our questions but to understand that not all of our questions are answered. Where there is silence, God fully expects us to obey what He has revealed. God is outraged when we fill in the silence with our own answers, speak for Him, or use these new answers as a rational to do something else, something more *reasonable*. No one has the authority to speak for God. Modern Christianity is broken, and one of the sins that broke it is the arrogance of religious leaders, who speak for the Lord and fill in the silence with their own answers. So, how does this relate to the *what if* scenarios concerning baptism? I'm glad you asked.

As stated earlier, the questions are more than fair, especially those that center on the individual who loves the Lord sincerely and is never baptized. I believe that every sincere student of God's word has wrestled with these issues, me included. From my study, this is what I believe are the scriptural responses to these scenarios. Yes, God expects everyone who desires to be His disciple to obey and believe His promise in Acts 2:38-39 and to repent and be baptized for the forgiveness of sins and the gift of the Holy Spirit. Yes, it is possible to be sincere and be sincerely wrong. The fact that someone's knowledge on this issue is in error or incomplete does not mean that their faith is not genuine, but just because someone's faith is sincere does not make them right. People that love Jesus can be sincerely wrong. So, what about the men and women, living and dead who have loved the Lord with full conviction and have not adhered to the pattern of New Testament baptism? Doesn't God make exceptions? Weren't they born again through their faith? Are these people lost or saved? Whether God has or does make exceptions is a matter that belongs to God and woe to the man who has the audacity to speak on matters that belong wholly to the Lord. If there are exceptions, they are God's to grant and if there is judgment, it is God's to give. What I know and trust is that our Lord will treat every individual with both grace and justice.

I have heard some teach that anyone who deviates from the Biblical model is surely lost, and I have known others to teach that the Lord surely allows faithful men and women into His kingdom regardless of baptism, reasoning that He would never keep someone out on a technicality. I submit that both schools of thought are clothed in arrogance. No man can speak for the one who made us, the one who speaks to things that are not as if they are. No man can speak for Him. We worship our Lord; we bow before Him; we tremble before Him, but only a fool speaks for Him. Let

God be God. Yes, I have opinions concerning all these questions, opinions that I largely keep to myself. Why? I understand that my opinions about salvation do not matter, but here is the thing, neither do theirs or yours. None of us gets a vote. God alone sits on the throne, and I trust that in every case He will do what is best.

Disciples are not the salvation police. We do not get to run around with our Bibles and tell people who is and who is not going to heaven. That is not our role, and frankly, that role is way above our pay grade. We are mailmen, and the gospel is the love letter we get to deliver. The mailman does not get to editorialize the mail. He just delivers it. If he delivers a notice that your rent is due, and you ask him, "I know that this says I need to pay the rent by tomorrow, but if I wait two weeks the landlord will make an exception, won't he?" All the mailman is going to do is wish you a nice day and distribute some more mail. That question is between you and the landlord. Maybe the landlord will make an exception and maybe he won't. The only thing that is sure is that if you pay the rent according to the notice, everything will be OK. Anything else is taking a risk. In our case, we can't get the author of the gospel on the phone and ask for an extension or an exception. Honestly, I do not know how the Lord has or will handle every situation. All I know for sure is that if someone repents and is baptized, he will be born again. His sins will be forgiven, and He will receive the Holy Spirit. This is a promise we can trust because the promise is for us, our children, and all who are far off, all who the Lord our God will call. I know that if someone obeys this command the Lord will keep His promise. Anything else is a risk, a risk I am not prepared to take and would not advise anyone to chance.

So, why chance it? That was the question I had to ask myself. What possible reason did I have for not obeying Acts 2:38? I had read the scriptures, they seemed clear, and at the end of the day, what did any of those scenarios have to do with me? Yes, it is possible to be sincerely wrong, but as the saying goes, when someone is confronted with the truth, he will either cease to be sincere or cease to be wrong. So, when I was confronted with a more complete understanding, what was I going to do? For me, baptism was a test. It was a test of the legitimacy of my surrender. Was Jesus truly Lord? Was His voice louder than the other voices in my life? Was I willing to humble myself and admit that some of my previous beliefs were wrong? Did I trust Jesus over the religious traditions that raised me? Was I willing to trust His promise over my own doubts and fears? As I prayed about my decision, staring back at me were the scriptures, none more prominently than Matthew 28:18-20.

Matthew 28:18-20

[18] Then Jesus came to them and said, "All authority in heaven and on earth has been given to me. [19] Therefore go and make disciples of all nations, baptizing them in the name of the Father and of the Son and of the Holy Spirit, [20] and teaching them to obey everything I have commanded you. And surely, I am with you always, to the very end of the age."

Matthew 28:18-20 is among Jesus's final instructions, and this passage makes it clear that baptism is very much part of His plan. When one has faith in Jesus and repents, deciding to turn from self and embrace discipleship, Jesus calls him to be baptized. An individual is not a candidate for baptism until he has decided to make Jesus Lord. But the question before me was how could I claim that Jesus was my Lord if I resisted the command to be baptized in His name? What would be my reason? Tradition? My pride? My fear? I was baptized in November on a weekday. I had spent most of the night reading scriptures and praying about my decision. I went to my classes, fidgety, already having decided what I was going to do. It was either a Tuesday or Thursday. There were no services scheduled at the church building where I had begun to worship. I did not have a car, and the building was over a half hour walk from campus. This was before the time of cell phones and the Internet, so advanced planning was extremely important, and I really did not have much of a plan other than urgency to obey what I had read. I had not thought it all through as far as the mechanics. I just started walking to the building the minute classes were over, determined to find someone in that building to baptize me. I showed up and spoke to the receptionist, who was able to locate the campus minister. He asked me a few questions, wanting to know if I understood the seriousness of my commitment and then asked if I wanted to wait and take more time to think about it. "No," I answered, "I'm ready. I want to be baptized, now." Now that I knew what Jesus wanted, I did not want another day to pass by outside of His promise. It was around 3:00PM. A few of my friends from the Bible study showed up, and minutes later, I was baptized. It was my wedding day, a special day. OK, honestly, I don't remember most of it. It was a blur, and I was an emotional mess. The one thing that I do remember and I will never forget is that I felt the presence of Jesus and His love, and I was determined to love him back with everything in me, and never let go...no turning back, no turning back.

Additional Scriptures Concerning Baptism

Additional Scriptures Concerning Baptism

Acts 2:36-39, John 3:3-6, Matthew 3:13-15,

Matthew 28:18-20, I Peter 3:20-21, Mark 16:16,

Colossians 2:11-12, Galatians 3:26-27, Romans 6:1-7,

Acts 8:26-40, Acts 9:17-19, Acts 22:15-16,

Acts 10:44-48, Acts16:13-15, Acts 16:31-34,

Acts 18:24-28, Acts 19:1-6, II Kings 5:1-19

Chapter 8

Meet the Family

Most people do not wait until after the wedding to meet their significant other's family. Generally, at some time during the courtship, normally after the relationship has become serious, the couple will meet each other's people. Michelle's mom loved me (hey, who wouldn't?), but my mom absolutely adored Michelle, and my wife became her adopted daughter. In fact, I honestly believe she liked Michelle a whole lot more than she liked me. I guess that could have made me feel insecure, but then we had children, and my mom doted on her granddaughters and totally forgot about both of us. That, my friends, is the circle of life. I share this because when we got married, we not only married one another; we became grafted into an extended family, in all its dysfunctional glory. Becoming a disciple is much like this.

When we are baptized into Christ, we are baptized into His family, and it is impossible to have a relationship with Christ without having one with His brothers and sisters. The idea that walking with God is purely vertical, just between the individual and God and nobody else, is foreign to the Bible. When we are born again, we are born into a brand new family. God is our father, Jesus is our brother, and every disciple is our brother or sister, and how we treat our brothers and sisters has a direct bearing on our relationship with God.

I John 4:20-21

[20] *Whoever claims to love God yet hates a brother or sister is a liar. For whoever does not love their brother and sister, whom they have seen, cannot love God, whom they have not seen.* [21] *And he has given us this*

command: Anyone who loves God must also love their brother and sister.

The scriptures make it clear that loving God also means loving God's people, His church. We have an obligation to the church and the church to us, but what exactly does that mean and how should that look? Fortunately, the Bible paints a vivid picture for us. But before we examine these scriptures, first we should define some terminology.

Ephesians 1:22-23

22 And God placed all things under his feet and appointed him to be head over everything for the church, 23 which is his body, the fullness of him who fills everything in every way

The Bible uses quite a few terms as synonyms for Christ's church, but among the most frequent is used here in Ephesians 1:22-23. This passage tells us that the church is not only Jesus's family; it is His body. So, frequently the word refers to the church as the body of Christ. What does the Bible teach us about Christ's body?

There is One Body

Ephesians 4:4-6

4 There is one body and one Spirit, just as you were called to one hope when you were called; 5 one Lord, one faith, one baptism; 6 one God and Father of all, who is over all and through all and in all.

This is a simple statement, but in a world with thousands, some say tens of thousands, of Christian denominations, it is also a radical one. There is only one body. Christ only has one church. Now, this statement does not mean that any congregation or fellowship of congregations can stake the claim of being the one true church. But what it is teaching is that Christ does not recognize denominations and man made divisions. He only has one family, and no one has the right to divide it. True Christianity cannot be divided up into brand names, as if someone is shopping for different types of peanut butter. Someone is either a disciple or he is not, and every true disciple of Christ is part of the same body and comprises Christ's church.

Not only does Ephesians 4:4-6 establish that Jesus only has one church; it defines the identity of that church. Just because someone claims to be a Christian, does not make him born again, and just because a church waves the Christian banner, does not mean it is a living, breathing congregation that belongs to Jesus. So how can one tell the difference? Christ's church is identified by its submission to one Lord, one faith, and one baptism. There should be an obvious devotion to the Lordship of Christ, holding faithfully to sound doctrine, and obedience to the practice of Jesus's baptism. Ephesians 4:4-6 lays out the general guiding principles that distinguish Christ's church and read in conjunction with Acts 2:42-47 a detailed description is conveyed concerning the DNA of a life giving church (for much more on this topic, I encourage you to purchase the *Love Story Workbook* and watch the videos about the body of Christ found in chapter eight). One thing is clear. While Jesus may not approve of or recognize denominational labels and man-made division, He very much cares about the spiritual make up of a congregation. As disciples, it matters where we attend church. Although no group is ever going to be perfect, it is important to connect to a congregation that is devoted to sound teaching and Biblical discipleship. Just picking the one closest to your house or the one with best music is probably not the best way to make such an important spiritual decision. It is important to choose prayerfully and choose well, and after a disciple has found a place to connect with God's people, the scriptures offer some instructions concerning how.

We Must Be Connected

I Corinthians 12:12-20

12 Just as a body, though one, has many parts, but all its many parts form one body, so it is with Christ. 13 For we were all baptized by one Spirit so as to form one body—whether Jews or Gentiles, slave or free—and we were all given the one Spirit to drink. **14** *Even so the body is not made up of one part but of many.*

15 *Now if the foot should say, "Because I am not a hand, I do not belong to the body," it would not for that reason stop being part of the body.* **16** *And if the ear should say, "Because I am not an eye, I do not belong to the body," it would not for that reason stop being part of the body.* **17** *If the whole body were an eye, where would the sense of hearing be? If the whole body were an ear, where would the sense of smell be?* **18** *But in fact God has placed the parts in the body, every one of them, just as he wanted them to be.* **19** *If they were all one part, where would the body be?* **20** *As it is, there are many parts, but one body.*

The church is the body of Christ. I Corinthians 12:12-20 makes it clear that the term body is not simply used as a metaphor for the church. It is a spiritual reality, and many of the rules that apply to our physical bodies apply to Jesus's spiritual one. Two points stand out from this passage: Every disciple needs the body, and every disciple is needed by the body.

I Corinthians 12:15-16 teaches us that just as parts of the human anatomy are interdependent and one part cannot function separate from the whole, no Christian can prosper outside of regular fellowship. As His disciple, Jesus desires to meet my needs, but the Church is His body, so when Jesus chooses to give me a hug, He often uses His church. When He wants to encourage me, inspire me, challenge me, teach me, mentor me, or reprimand me, He frequently uses the parts of the body. Through individual relationships, through small groups, and through corporate worship, Jesus is constantly speaking to me, and if I let myself be too busy or too distracted to assemble with His saints, I shut off one of the primary methods that Christ speaks to me and touches me. No Christian has ever become more spiritual by neglecting fellowship or treating Sunday services as a movie, where he sees the show, pays his money, and leaves. We need the body, but like with many things, we get out what we put in. If a disciple invests little, he grows little. If he invests much, he'll grow abundantly. Neglecting it all together is like cutting off the pinky from the hand. Nothing good will come from it. We need the body and the body needs us.

So, as a brand new, baby Christian, it was easy for me to see how I needed the body. Everything was new to me. Every Bible study, campus devotional, and worship service taught me something new, and the time I spent being mentored by more mature Christians was invaluable. I understood how I needed them. How did they need me?

We all have a role, each and every one of us. We have unique gifts, talents, and perspectives. In addition, our journey, with all of its successes, failures, joy, and pain, is something strictly our own. Whether I felt it or not, I was special and designed with specific purpose and had an ordained role to play in building up Christ's body that was exclusively mine, and that was as true as a one day old Christian as it is thirty–four years into my story. Even way back then, there were needs in the congregation that I was created to fill, people that I was there to encourage, individuals who my journey would inspire, and problems that my unique perspective was adept at identifying. As time went on, I gradually noticed issues and needs and sometimes wondered why not everyone saw what I was seeing. It finally dawned on me that God had allowed me to see these things because He wanted me to do something to help. I could either sit in the back of the church and be critical, or I could be part of the solution, more importantly be part of my Lord's plan. I was a member of Christ's body. When Jesus desired to give a hug, he would use me if I let him. When He wanted to address a need, reprimand sin, mentor the lost, or encourage the hurting, He would speak through me. I was there for a reason. This is equally true for each and every disciple of Christ. For disciples, church is not just something that we attend. We are the church. We are a family of imperfect, surrendered souls bound by grace, our love for the Lord, and our love for one another. As each part does its work, the body grows and prospers, and more light is spread into this dark world.

Additional Scriptures Concerning the Church

Acts 2:42-47, John 13:34-35, Ephesians 1:22-23,

Ephesians 2:19-22, I Corinthians 12:12-26, Romans 12:3-13,

Hebrews 10:23-25, Matthew 18:18-20, Matthew 6:33,

Colossians 1:17-18, I Corinthians 1:10-13, II Timothy 4:1-5,

Chapter 9

Next Steps

So, I met Michelle, got to know her, fell madly in love, met her family, and somehow, conned her into marrying me. So, was that the end of our story? Hardly. Twenty-nine years later and we're still going strong. It has been a wild ride. No, the wedding wasn't the end. It was the end of the beginning. My journey with Jesus has been the same. My baptism was the end of one life and the start of another, something better. It ushered in a new chapter of my adventure, and I've been learning to live a spirit-filled life ever since. So, now that we've reached this point in our story, what are the next steps? Thankfully, for this too, the Lord left instructions.

Matthew 28:18-20

18 Then Jesus came to them and said, "All authority in heaven and on earth has been given to me. 19 Therefore go and make disciples of all nations, baptizing them in the name of the Father and of the Son and of the Holy Spirit, 20 and teaching them to obey everything I have commanded you. And surely, I am with you always, to the very end of the age."

As stated earlier, I've been blessed with being married to Michelle, an amazing woman of God, for almost three decades, and we have two beautiful daughters. I know this is all from God. Left on my own, with my sinful nature and emotional baggage, none of this would have been possible. I know something else. Without the men who took me under their wing during my first two years as a Christian, my life would have been very different. They were there when I was most vulnerable, when my faith was new and untested. These brothers were obeying Matthew 28:18-20, particularly verse 20, not simply teaching me about discipleship and baptizing me but staying involved in my life and leading me to spiritual maturity. For a young disciple, being mentored is an important next step, and for mature disciples, it is important to be a mentor and give back what has been given to you. Spiritual maturity, learning to become disciples who make disciples, is the goal. If you are interested in building on the lessons learned from this book, I have five scripture inspired next steps to recommend.

1. **Stay in Prayer and Bible Study:** The most significant decision that you can make to aid in your spiritual growth is to walk with Jesus daily. It should be your first priority to have daily conversations with the Lord, talking to Him and listening to Him. Remember, prayer and obedience is how we speak to God, and the word is the primary way that He speaks to us. Make time, daily, to speak and listen. Tools can help. Hopefully, this book has served as a useful tool. In addition, there are two other books that I can recommend: The *Love Story Workbook* and *Passing It On*. The *Love Story Workbook* is a companion book that will help personalize the lessons found in Love Story. Comprised of practical, thought provoking questions and studies, the workbook offers unique insights as well as links to the Love Story Videos. The lessons and videos have proven to be extremely beneficial to many people. *Passing It On* is a series of studies that can serve as either devotional times or a study guide for a mentor and student. Both books can be found at the website www.jesuslovestory.com

2. **Find a Church:** If you have not done so, find and connect with a church devoted to disciple making and sound Biblical teaching. Study Acts 2:42-47 and other scriptures concerning the body/Christ's church and seek a church committed to the Biblical

model. If you currently attend a church but feel it is not devoted to these principles, please, do not hesitate to look for another. Finding a life giving body of believers is one of the most important investments you can make for your spiritual journey.

3. **Find a Mentor:** Depending on where you are in your spiritual journey, it is important to find a mentor or become one. Matthew 28:18-20 shows that spiritual mentorship is part of God's plan. Look for someone who is a true disciple of Jesus, not simply knowledgeable and religious. In our broken world, disciples have a tendency to stand out. Seek someone who has a solid grasp on the word, whose righteousness and walk are inspiring, and who has a desire to invest in you. This can be one of the most rewarding relationships of your life. Equally important is that after you have reached a level of spiritual maturity, that you find someone to mentor. Discipleship is designed to be a gift that keeps on giving.

4. **Share What You Know:** You don't have to be a Bible expert to share what you do know and what God has done for you. We are commanded to go, and there is no time like the present to put that command into practice. Share your knowledge, share the tools that have blessed you, and share your story. God can use you where you are today to be a blessing to someone else.

5. **Tell Us Your Story:** If *Love Story* has been a blessing to your life, we want to hear about and share your story. Email us at thejesuslovestory@gmail.com with your written or video testimonials, and we will post as many as possible on our website www.jesuslovestory.com and on social media.

If you are ready to be Jesus' disciple, prepare for the greatest adventure of your life. As Jesus's co-workers, we get to be curse breakers. Sin is the gift that keeps on giving, but so is love. But here is the key: to make a difference, you must risk something; to change the world, you must risk everything. Go and together let us share the *Love Story* to a broken world, helping it be a little less broken one story at a time.

Bibliography

Coleman, Robert E. The Master Plan of Evangelism 2nded.Grand Rapids: Fleming H. Revell a division of Baker Book House Company, 1963.

Anton, Edward J. Repentance: A Cosmic Shift of Mind & Heart Waltham: Discipling Publications International, 2005

Jacoby, Dr. Douglas (2013, July 31). *A (more accurate) Medical Account of the Crucifixion* Retrieved Fromhttps://www.douglasjacoby.com/a-more-accurate-medical-account-of-the-crucifixion/

Davis, Dr. C. Truman. *A Physicians View of the Crucifixion of Jesus Christ* Retrieved Fromhttp://www1.cbn.com/medical-view-of-the-crucifixion-of-jesus-christ

McClister, David (2000, January). *The Scourging of Jesus*http://www.truthmagazine.com/archives/volume44/v440106010.htm

Driscoll, Mark (2014, April 4). *How Much Did Jesus Suffer? A Medical Account of Death by Crucifixion* Retrieved From https://www.charismanews.com/opinion/43525-how-much-did-jesus-suffer-a-medical-account-of-death-by-crucifixion

All About God.com (2002-2017) *What is Sin* Retrieved From https://www.allaboutgod.com/what-is-sin.htm

Ybarra, Thomas, R. (2014, April 14). *Repentance On Sunday for What One Has Done on Saturday* Retrieved From https://quoteinvestigator.com/2014/04/14/repent-day/

Zavada, Jack (2017 March 6). *Repentance: What Is Repentance in Christianity?* Retrieved From https://www.thoughtco.com/what-is-repentance-700694/

Trotter, Andrew, H., Jr. *Grace* Retrieved From https://www.biblestudytools.com/dictionary/grace/

Fairchild, Mary (2017 June 28). *Definition of God's Grace: What Does God's Grace Mean to Christians?* Retrieved From https://www.thoughtco.com/meaning-of-gods-grace-for-christians-700723

Jacoby, Dr. Douglas (2016 January 28). *Baptism Basics (Part I)* Retrieved From http://www.disciplestoday.org/bible-study/digging-deeper/item-7705-douglas-jacoby-baptism-part-1#.WlPFzyOZO7Y

Lotha, Gloria (2009, May 5). *Legion* Retrieved From https://www.britannica.com/topic/legion

The Hebrew-Greek Key Word Study Bible. Chattanooga: AMG Publishers, 1996

CPSIA information can be obtained
at www.ICGtesting.com
Printed in the USA
FFOW01n2352080418
46192928-47455FF